The Last
"TRUE"
ROLLER
DERBY

The Last "TRUE" ROLLER DERBY

A MEMOIR

Larry Smith

THE LAST "TRUE" ROLLER DERBY
A MEMOIR

iUniverse books may be ordered through booksellers or by contacting:

iUniverse
1663 Liberty Drive
Bloomington, IN 47403
www.iuniverse.com
1-800-Authors (1-800-288-4677)

Because of the dynamic nature of the Internet, any web addresses or links contained in this book may have changed since publication and may no longer be valid. The views expressed in this work are solely those of the author and do not necessarily reflect the views of the publisher, and the publisher hereby disclaims any responsibility for them.

Any people depicted in stock imagery provided by Thinkstock are models, and such images are being used for illustrative purposes only. Certain stock imagery © Thinkstock.

ISBN: 978-1-4917-8015-2 (sc)
ISBN: 978-1-4917-8017-6 (hc)
ISBN: 978-1-4917-8016-9 (e)

Library of Congress Control Number: 2015918226

Print information available on the last page.

iUniverse rev. date: 01/12/2016

CONTENTS

A TRUE DAMON RUNYON STORY

What could be more fitting than a real Damon Runyon story? After all, it was Leo Seltzer and Damon Runyon who came up with the idea of a game fashioned after the six-day bicycle races. However, in this new game, the men and women of the same team competed equally, and their scores, added together, determined the winner of the match. Leo and Damon drew up the game on a tablecloth in a New York City restaurant after they viewed a sample of the six-day bicycle races. Please keep in mind that prior to the 1940s, women had different sets of rules for sports. In basketball, ladies were only allowed to dribble the ball twice before shooting or passing. They performed shots on the goal by bending at the waist, holding the ball in both hands between their knees, and then, with both hands, throwing the ball toward the basket. It sounds a little dorky, and it was. In those days, women could not play football or baseball without people whispering and talking about how improper it was.

This was about the same time that World War II was raging in Europe. Most Americans were still feeling the pain of the Great Depression. Women were just starting to replace men in factories as the guys went off to fight the war. So the time was ripe for the Roller Derby to be born. The sport was constantly changing, trying to find its following. The movie *Fireball*, starring none other than Mickey Rooney, shows how the game was played in the beginning. As the game evolved in the 1960s through mid-1970s, it became faster, using a smaller track and different skates and wheels. This new game was designed for television. In the early days, the Roller Derby was big stuff. However, the story was always the same: good triumphed over evil. The home team always skated cleanly without mayhem, while the visiting team, wearing the darker jerseys, would do anything to win. Ultimately, the clean-cut skater who followed the rules would finally take on the bully to win the game.

This Damon Runyon story was true because it was about me. As you may know by now, I have a big ego. I lived the part of the poor boy from nowhere who left home at sixteen to escape an alcoholic father who had a hard time keeping a job. My stepmother patiently nurtured her two kids and me while hedgehopping all over the western United States in an effort to keep our little family together. Normally, we moved three or four times each year. Usually, I would be dropped off at my grandmother's home or my aunt Ruth's. These so-called visits often spanned a couple of weeks while my dad found a new job. The drill was always the same: my grandmother and aunt would fight to keep me with them, but my dad would always insist that I was his kid and would be better off with him.

You can imagine the emotional baggage these experiences created. I began stuttering and allowing bullies to push me around, until I'd finally had enough. I started calling out the local bully during my first few days at a new school. Though I was a skinny little kid, I started fighting back, inflicting some damage on the local bullies. They finally started leaving me alone. As a matter of fact, because of my challenges, the bully crowd would suddenly make me their friend. Then they would start to pull that crap on some other skinny kid. I would then stick up for the kid, ending my friendship with the bullies. You see, I was a natural for the Roller Derby.

Let's jump ahead to 1963, when I lived in Hayward, California, and worked for Golden Gate Drywall out of Redwood City. I still had a dream that I would someday join the Roller Derby. My Sheetrock-hanging partner, Bill Helms, came to work one Monday looking as if he had been mugged. One eye was black, he had a couple of scratches on his face, and he was limping. I asked what had happened, and he told me he had gone to the Roller Derby Training School in Oakland, California, over the weekend. He had not only gotten injured while trying to skate on the banked track but also gotten into a fistfight with a couple of the trainees. Knowing Bill, he probably started the fight, and he certainly gave them a go—Bill was one tough guy.

You can only imagine how I was feeling. I had bragged for a few years that I was going to join the Roller Derby. Although I had no idea there was an active Roller Derby team in my backyard—the San Francisco Bay Area Bombers—I discovered that the Roller Derby had split into two factions: the International Roller Derby League (IRDL), headed by Jerry Seltzer (son of Leo Seltzer, the Roller Derby founder), and Roller Games of Southern California, led by Bill Griffith, a local promoter.

It was a long week waiting until Saturday so that I could go to the school and check out how to join the Roller Derby. Had I known, I would have attended the weeknight training sessions to watch others train. Instead, I sat in my little apartment, exercising in order to get into fighting shape. Saturday finally came. I was in line, waiting for school to begin, when the door flew open, and a rather large, overweight guy with a giant cigar hanging from his mouth swaggered in, looking like a gangster I had seen in the movies. This school was a former auto-repair garage and had a concrete floor, skylights, and a little shack-like structure that served as the owner's office, in addition to small dressing rooms attached to the office. It was not painted, and it was dirty.

I spent months training every night after work and on weekends. It seemed I was always at the training facility. The Roller Derby bug bit me big-time, and George and Ernie knew it. They were responsible for getting me a tryout with the Los Angles Roller Games, and subsequently, I secured a job in Phoenix, Arizona, skating for Ernie Mohame's semipro team. The Los Angeles guys wanted me to skate on their minor-league team until I was discovered. However, I went back to George's school and skated at Kezar Pavilion in San Francisco before the Bay Bombers began televising the big game of the week on Sunday afternoons.

I only skated about ten minor-league games before the 1963 play-offs at the San Francisco Cow Palace. I was working as a carpenter in San Francisco, so I could have afforded the price of the tickets to the play-offs, but in pure Damon Runyon style, I elected to take the hawking job that the concessionaire of the Cow Palace offered me. That's right—I would be selling the official Roller Derby programs while watching the games. The following year, I wasn't selling programs, but I was receiving Rookie of the Year honors as a member of the IRDL and the Chicago Pioneers.

My dream had come true.

WHY I'M WRITING THE ROLLER DERBY STORY

I have given this a lot of thought. I left the Roller Derby in late 1973 to become a Realtor, though I did accept a few games in 1974 and 1975. I hope the way I have presented this subject is acceptable to all the fans who love the game and travel four hundred to five hundred miles to attend matches in their area, come rain or shine, sleet or snow. Those are the fans I hope to reach with this book. My goal is to write about topics, incidents, and stories of my life in the Roller Derby—in particular, the road trips. This is American history. I was fortunate to live it.

The stories are taken from memory. Sometimes the dates may be incorrect, and the skaters' names may be wrong. However, the gist of the story will always be in the spirit of truth and goodwill. I will strive to write the stories, and God willing, I will finish them before being called to that game in heaven. What a glorious reunion that will be!

WHAT ATTRACTED ME TO THE ROLLER DERBY

Girls, skating, and Hawaii—and let's not forget the big bucks.

When I was twelve years old, we lived in San Bernardino, California, for a while. My parents started watching the T-Birds from Roller Games around the same time when a movie starring Mickey Rooney, *Fireball*, was out. I watched the movie as well as the Roller Derby. I became an avid fan.

Only one problem presented itself: I couldn't skate a lick. I loved baseball and football but gave them up to concentrate on skating. I worked for my father and uncles in the building trades on weekends. I saved up my earnings, cut some lawns, and bought myself a pair of clip-on street skates. After a few weeks and many bruises and sidewalk burns, I became confident enough to go to a roller rink. I was completely hooked.

Since my family moved three to four times a year in search of work, I attended a lot of new schools in new towns with new roller rinks, where I discovered that girls were cool. Additionally, I learned to skate roller-hockey as well, which provided me with instant friends. This was also cool.

Whenever someone asked me what I wanted to do when I grew up, I always answered, "I'm going to join the Roller Derby." This usually earned me strange looks and occasionally amused smiles.

At age sixteen, I left home, or I should say that home left me. We were living on a farm in Alta Vista, Kansas, and my dad was working in construction, building homes at Fort Riley, along with one of my uncles. One night, I ran away, hiding out until my parents finished loading up their trailer for the move back to California. My uncle took me in, allowing me to work with him in construction and help out on his small farm. While working, I was able to stay in school at Alta Vista High School, and I graduated in 1962. At the end of the summer, I moved to Emporia, Kansas, to attend Kansas State University's engineering program. However, the Roller Derby itch was pulling me inexorably to the skating rink.

In 1963, I moved back to California and lived in San Leandro while working as a carpenter in San Francisco. One of my carpenter buddies came to work looking like he had been mugged. It turned out that he had. While attending George "GK" Koudounis's 105th Avenue Roller Derby Training Center in Oakland, he'd gotten into a fistfight with a couple of trainees who knew how to fight better than he did. I was surprised by this since he was a tough guy. The next weekend, I started training at GK's Roller Derby school.

Sometime in early 1964, since I hadn't been picked up by any of the San Francisco teams, I convinced GK to recommend me for a tryout with the Los Angeles teams. George told me to go to the Olympic arena in Los Angles, where the T-Birds were skating, and ask for Russ Massro, who agreed to give me a tryout. After quitting my job, I drove down to Southern California and attended a game. When I told the box office manager that George had sent me, he said, "Who?" and "Who are you?" After I did some talking and pleading, he asked a member of the team staff to come out after the game to interview me. I don't remember who he was, but he finally let me take about ten laps around the track. After a couple of falls and a couple of rails, he told me I could join their training school and that maybe after a few months, I might improve enough to be selected for one of the visiting teams.

I returned to GT's school with my tail between my legs, but now I knew I was destined to skate professionally. GT told me about a group in Phoenix that wanted four guys and two girls to skate for them. I spoke to George, telling him that I would recruit the people he needed and that we would all arrive ready to skate in a few days. With George's help, we all piled into my old 1950 Chevy coupe and drove to Phoenix. I don't remember their names, except for Dorothy Lee, the 1965 Rookie of the Year winner for the San Francisco Bay Bombers. After arrival, we boarded with Ernie Mohamad's wrestling group in Old Town Phoenix.

We skated two or three games a week at a car racetrack outside in the cold. We were paid twenty dollars a game, and we almost starved. After a few weeks, Ernie purchased an old Safeway store and turned it into an arena complete with bleachers, two dressing rooms, and a wrestling ring in the middle of the derby track. We alternated skating nights with the wrestlers; I even got to do a match race with Tito Copa and his bear. I convinced Ernie to let me run a training school on Saturdays to train new skaters, hoping to increase revenue. We charged novice skaters $1.50 for the privilege of receiving professional instruction from ten o'clock in the morning until two o'clock in the afternoon. Ernie's cut was one dollar per person, while I cashed in at fifty cents per head. More than two hundred skaters showed up the first weekend. That night, the six of us went to a diner for steak dinners. Man, were we hungry!

We skated against teams from Los Angeles, and the matches were televised locally. After averaging a meager seven hundred people a night for several months, we finally called it quits and went home. After a few more weeks in GK's school, Bert Wall, coach of the Hawaiian Pioneers, arrived to recruit a couple of skaters for an upcoming road trip starting in January 1965. Of course I said, "Yes! When do I leave?" After all, who could resist living in Hawaii while getting paid to skate? *Wow, a dream come true!* I thought. In early January, Ken Monte, coach of the Red Devils, came by and picked me up. He already had Sue Figulia along with a few other skaters in his car. Together, we all headed to Denver, Omaha, St. Louis, and Chicago, with stops in a few small towns in between. The first night in Denver, they gave me a Chicago Pioneer uniform. I said, "Chicago!" The Hawaiian team was now Bill Griffith's Roller Games team. So much for Hawaii. It would be another fourteen years before I finally made it to Hawaii, but it was worth the wait.

So my answer to your question "What attracted me to join the Roller Derby?" is "Girls, skating, and Hawaii, and don't forget the big bucks!"

BARROOM FIGHT AT THE HOLIDAY INN IN CHICAGO

In January 1965, after two weeks on the road, we arrived at the Holiday Inn in East Chicago, Illinois. We had two whole days off. At the time, I was only a nineteen-year-old rookie in the Roller Derby. My roommates, Dave Cannella and Ken Kunzelman, treated me like a brother, generously offering me advice on how to stay out of trouble. The first night, Dave and Ken headed to the bar, telling me to stay put. I was not even to go down to the lobby, because this hotel was not only in a bad section of town but also known for brawling truck drivers and longshoremen. I didn't really understand what they meant, but I had seen tough guys in the movies and knew I'd be wise to do what Dave and Ken told me—at least for now. You will read about my fake ID as well as my night in jail a bit later.

After watching some fuzzy black-and-white TV, I decided to go down to the lobby to get a candy bar and a couple of soft drinks. The door to the bar was open, so I peeked in. Keep in mind that this was 1965, and this was a hotel housing bigots and racists from the Deep South. I don't remember exactly who was there, but I saw several of our black female skaters sitting on barstools next to Dave, Ken, and a few other white skaters. The noise from the jukebox was deafening, but I could still hear the racial slurs coming from a group of thugs in the corner. All of a sudden, a couple of large dudes went over to the black female skaters and started spewing racially charged words at them. About that time, our male skaters stood up and started punching the dudes. It was then that the other racist thugs jumped in. Before I knew it, one was coming my way. A swift kick to his nuts changed his mind; those karate lessons really paid off. About that time, I saw one of the truckers knock one of the women from her barstool, and now all the girls were throwing punches. The one who'd been knocked down got up with a Coca-Cola bottle in her hand and laid one guy out with a crack in his skull. He dropped as if he had been shot dead. Fortunately for her, he wasn't dead, just out cold.

Suddenly, someone started yelling, "The cops are here!" and everyone started running. Dave Cannella and Jimmy Pierce, our truck driver, grabbed me, and we headed for the stairs to our third-floor room. Once we got there, Dave opened the door and said, "Get in, and keep quiet. Do not open the door for any reason. If there is a fire, jump out the window." Of course, I didn't think he really meant that—at least I hoped he didn't. A couple of minutes after Dave took off, I heard someone running down the hall, yelling, "He's got a gun!" Stupid me—I opened the door and looked out into the hallway. One of our female skaters shouted, "Get back inside, and stay there!"

I wasn't sleepy anymore—I was scared crapless. After what seemed like hours, Dave and Kenny came back to the room, laughing and recounting the excitement of the night. It seems that a friend of the thug who got the Coke-bottle haircut had said he was a "made guy." Even I knew what that meant in Chicago. He was determined to kill whoever had hit his friend with the Coke bottle. But before he could do anything, the cops arrested him on an outstanding warrant.

After the cops left, everyone settled down. Even the truckers began dancing with our skaters and vice versa. It seems that females didn't customarily hang out in this bar, and the prospect of getting laid was more important to them than their bigotry. What the truckers didn't know was that the girls hanging out in the bar were lesbians. Our next time in town, we went to the Cicero Bar, and I ended up in jail, but that's another story.

A NIGHT IN A CHICAGO JAIL

That's right—I spent a night in a Chicago jail. After being on the road for a few weeks, we finally returned to Chicago and got a night off. Before skating at the famed Chicago Coliseum with ghosts, muddy floors, and a building that should have been demolished, I failed to heed Ken Monte's warning not to go drinking at the Cicero Club. However, it was a skater's tradition to get drunk at the Cicero Club. After all, we hadn't had a real day off in weeks. There I was, in the heart of the Cicero section of Chicago. This was a mobster town. The history is incredible. First, the coliseum we would be skating in had once been used to house Southern rebels from the Civil War. The place was haunted. It had a floor that would sweat when the crowds arrived and then turn muddy. The mud stuck to our wheels, making it hard to skate. This building, packed to the rafters, would shake when the crowd got excited. But most fascinating were the stories about the Mafia and the famous Cicero Club, which was reported to be a mobster hangout. They loved the skaters, so who in his right mind would not go have a drink?

My roommate, Dave Cannella, was from Missouri and had two driver's licenses, and neither one had photos. I told him I wanted to go to the club, but since I was only nineteen years old, my license would be no help if I was carded. Dave mentioned he had two licenses, and both were lying on his bed while he took a shower and got ready to party. When we left for the club, I had Dave's extra license, and of course, he didn't know anything about it.

When we got to the club, it was nearly full, crowded with skaters and other people whom I assumed must be mobsters. Dave and I found two barstools together, sat down, and ordered two beers. As soon as the beers were served, two Chicago policemen walked in and started checking IDs. Dave and I turned our backs to each other, and one cop asked Dave for his license, while the other asked for mine. As the policeman checked out our credentials, the policeman talking with Dave said, "So, Mr. Cannella, how long will you be in Chicago?" Dave told him he was a skater and was there for the Roller Derby.

About that time, my cop asked me the same thing: "So, Mr. Cannella, how long will you be in Chicago?" The two cops simultaneously looked at each other, and one said, "Two Mr. Cannellas. Are you brothers?" I said yes. By this time, the cops were comparing the licenses, and one said, "You are both named David Cannella?" Well, by this time, I knew I was in trouble, so I told the cops I had stolen Dave's second ID and that he didn't know anything about it. Dave's policeman asked Dave if that was the truth. Now, keep in mind that Dave could have gone to jail for a long time for contributing to the delinquency of a minor, so I spoke up again, assuring the cops that my stealing his license had put him in this spot. Dave finally reluctantly agreed and said he had no knowledge of my true age and had not given me his spare license.

So off to jail I went. I was scared to death. I had never been in jail and didn't know what to expect other than what movies and TV shows portrayed. Plus, since I had broken the rules, I knew Ken Monte could fire me and leave me to rot in that Chicago jail. After the booking and fingerprinting, the police took my shoes, my belt, and all my other personal belongings. I was led into a jail cell and left alone with my thoughts. I could handle being alone. I knew it was safer than having Bruno as my cell mate. However, my solitary bliss didn't last long. Within a few minutes, they deposited another young man in my cell. He looked to be in his early twenties and told me he was in for car theft. He had a set of master keys that he'd managed to sneak into the cell, and he wanted me to hold them since the police hadn't completed his frisking and would soon be back to do so. Since this kid was at least six feet tall and more than two hundred pounds, I reluctantly agreed. I didn't need a jailhouse fight on my record too. As soon as I put the keys in my pocket, a jailer came by and took the kid away. Now I had the master keys to help me steal cars, and God knows what else they could have accused me of if they'd frisked me again. I didn't sleep a wink all night.

Early in the morning, I was let out of my cell and taken to a holding room where I would wait for my arraignment. Thank God they had coffee—hot and black. When I went into the courtroom, I saw Ken Monte with a scowl that would have scared Count Dracula. The court clerk read the charges, and the judge asked me how I pleaded. Keep in mind that this was 1964, and I don't believe the reading of Miranda rights was required. I had no attorney, and apparently, the charges were reduced to a misdemeanor. Thankfully, Ken Monte had paid my bail.

I pleaded guilty, and the judge told me that since Mr. Monte had paid my bail, I was free to go. However, I had to report back in a few weeks for a hearing, which of course I agreed to do, believing I was going to be fired and would never set foot in Illinois again. Ken never said a word. He drove me back to the hotel, and I went straight up to my room. Later, Dave asked about my night in jail, and within a few minutes, various skaters dropped by to hear the details of my ordeal. I felt like a hero or something. I was part of the crowd. I was on the team but still thought Ken Monte would probably fire me in front of the team in the middle of the dressing room either before or after the game.

It was a strange night. When I got to the game, it was as if I wasn't there. No one talked with me or acknowledged me in the dressing room, on the track, or even during the game. Even though I was scoring points, getting beat up, and participating in all the other normal derby happenings no one would talk to me. When the game was over, I headed to the dressing room, and I knew this was it. Ken would fire me in front of everyone, and I would be sent to the bus station with my bag in hand. However, Ken didn't mention anything about my being fired, and no one spoke to me.

Back at the hotel, I stayed in my room. Dave was at the club with everyone else, and before he returned, I went to bed and slept until the alarm went off. That morning, as I got ready, neither Dave nor I talked about the impending firing I believed would surely happen before the team left for St. Louis. When I got to Ken's car, the other two skaters were already seated, and the trunk was open, so I threw my suitcase in the trunk, closed the lid, and climbed into the backseat. No one said a word. It was silent all the way to St. Louis—about a seven-hour drive. When we arrived at our hotel, Ken pulled the car in and parked. The other skaters got out, took their bags, and walked into the lobby, while Ken stood by the car. As I started to go inside, Ken stopped me. I thought to myself, *Here it is. I'm going to get fired.*

He started to smile and then said, "If you ever do something that stupid again or even break a rule, you will be going home." He then walked inside the lobby and got the key to his room. Dumbfounded, I went to my room. That night, in the dressing room and during the game, everything was back to normal. However, I did get the nickname Jailbird for a couple of weeks.

I never did go for the hearing the next time we were in Chicago. From then on, every time we played in Chicago, I would constantly look over my shoulder, expecting the cops to arrest me.

DRAFT DODGER IN DENVER, OR HOW TO GET TO LEAVENWORTH WITHOUT REALLY TRYING

In 1965, after several months on the road, we played Denver, Colorado, again, and I was excited. During my last trip there, I'd recorded my highest score for a single game: fifteen points. I'd scored the winning points by jumping the fallen pack in the final two seconds of the game with two opposing jammers on my tail. The score had gone back and forth, with the Chicago Pioneer girls getting within one point of the Denver Red Devils when they turned the game over to the boys for the last period.

On the last play, the Red Devils were ahead by two points, when I broke away from the pack with a strong whip from Bert Wall, our coach and my mentor. Two of the Red Devils were hot on my tail, and I knew Bert would try to subway the pack as I came in. If only I could shake the two Devils on my tail, I could score three before the two jammers caught up to me. I was fast but not that fast. I decided to do a layout, something I had seen in old Roller Derby plays. It was seldom used. I had to sucker the two Devils in close, getting them side by side on the straightaway so that I could jump in the air as they closed in on me and lay my body out lengthwise from the rail to the infield, catching them in the chest, causing them to fall. Then I rolled forward off them to get on my feet and beat them to the end of the pack to score by jumping the pack, which by now had been subwayed by Bert and the rest of our team. Then I called off the jam before the Devils could score again. The play worked perfectly, and we won.

But that's not the point of this story. I loved Denver and was looking for a repeat. On my last visit, I'd hooked up with a couple of the local girls after the game, and we had a great time. Well, this time, as I arrived at the arena to set up the track, the building manager warned me that there were two FBI agents looking for me. My first thought was that the girls might have been too young and that I was in trouble. I called Bert Wall and asked him what I should do. He thought for a few moments and then advised me to hide out in the dressing room until he could come down to the building and question the FBI agents. I followed his advice, but it seemed like hours before finally Bert showed up. He had spent some time calling our headquarters in Oakland, California, to see if they had heard anything. No one seemed to know what this was about.

This was 1965, and the Vietnam War was going full bore. Several skaters had already been drafted, but that wasn't in my thoughts at the time. Finally, Bert went to the arena manager's office and asked to speak to the two FBI agents, but they were out on the arena floor, questioning the other skaters on my whereabouts. They, of course, told the feds I was in the dressing room. Before Bert could cut them off, they came into the dressing room, asking for Larry Smith. Fortunately, I told them who I was and asked them what was going on. They said I was listed as a draft dodger, and they were there to escort me back to Oakland, California, where I would be inducted into the army. About that time, Bert Wall and Hal Janowitz, a former skater and our road manager, came in and tried to reason with the FBI guys. After a few tense moments and a lot of explanation, we were able to convince the government guys that I had not received my draft notices and had not thrown them away. It took a couple of calls to our headquarters to locate the undelivered draft notices, which were found in a back room. In those days, mail for the rookies was the last to be forwarded. We were often two or three weeks behind in getting our mail delivered. That changed shortly after this incident.

We were finally able to convince the agents that I wasn't a flight risk and would accompany them to Oakland the following morning. I planned to take my physical the morning after arriving; however, the agents hardly left my side. They stayed in the dressing room with me, went to dinner with the crew, and followed me to and from the track. They even waited while I showered. Then they followed me back to the motel so that I could get my clothes before heading to the airport for a 2:00 a.m. flight to Oakland. After traveling with me on the plane, they deposited me in a cheap hotel across from the induction center. I thought the surveillance would stop at the Oakland Hotel, but to my surprise, they were waiting for me the next morning as I walked across the street to get my preinduction physical.

You would have thought I was a hardened criminal. The feds announced to the motel staff that I had been apprehended in Denver for draft dodging and that they would need to keep a guard on me until they determined if I could be drafted. The physical was going well, and I knew I would be in Fort Ord, California, by the end of the day. After eight weeks of whipping my already-hard body into shape, I would become a fighting machine for the USA.

During a short break, I managed to phone my physician, Dr. Robert Moore, to ask for help. One of my knees had taken a pounding in Denver, and I hadn't been wearing the knee brace Dr. Moore had prescribed. As a result, I had water on the knee, and my knee was obviously swollen. I hoped it might disqualify me from military service. When I explained to the army doctor about my knee and its condition, as well as the requirement to wear a knee brace during any strenuous exercise, he asked to speak with Dr. Moore. Thank God Dr. Moore made a convincing argument that I was not fit for active military duty. After that ordeal, I would need at least a few weeks off to heal and would possibly need surgery on my knee.

Don't get me wrong. If I had been inducted, I would have served, fought, and died if that were God's will. But since I had a legitimate out, I was determined to use it. The army doctor classified me as 4-R, not 4-F. The 4-R designation meant that in a few months, I would be reevaluated. If my knee had healed sufficiently, I would be moved to the head of the line for induction into the US Army.

I found it amazing that government officials never asked me what I did for a living. On all my paperwork I filled out when registering for the draft, I reported my occupation as a carpenter. I made no mention of the Roller Derby or the fact that a couple of nights prior, I had been skating around a high-banked track going thirty-plus miles per hour with my hair on fire, jumping, blocking, and even fighting. Had the doctors at the induction center known this, I think I would have been on my way to Vietnam in a heartbeat.

After completing the preinduction examination, I jumped on the first bus headed to Portland, Oregon, so that I could rejoin the team. For the next few months, I waited for the dreaded letter that would send me back to the induction center to begin my life in the army. However, it never happened—no letter, no FBI guys. Nothing. I went on to skate for another ten years without incident or contact from the draft board. After the war ended, I always felt a little guilty for not having served when called upon.

ROAD TRIPS AND MY THOUGHTS ON TURNPIKES

The East Coast is famous for their turnpikes, and the West Coast could learn a lesson from their success. Yes, you have to pay to travel on them, but they are well kept and have adequate rest stops with restaurants and inns just off the exits. Here in California, we pay for bad roads with few rest stops via gasoline and sales taxes. If California adopted the turnpike concept, I believe we would be able to travel on better roads and have fewer accidents due to fatigued drivers.

One of the turnpikes—or, as the Canadians call them, toll roads—might be a little overdone in the Montreal-to-Granby run. The total trip from Montreal to Granby is less than ninety miles, but they have eight tollbooths, as you cross eight county lines, and each county has its own tollbooth. Now, that is overdoing it! But the road is in great condition, and the snow-removal equipment is there to keep that roadway clear.

Normally, during the first week of January, our road trip would take us from the San Francisco Bay Area through the southwestern states, the midwestern states, and the eastern seaboard and southern states into the northwestern states. Then we'd reverse our course back to the Bay Area. Usually, this would leave us ending our road trip a few thousand miles away from home in mid-May. Those lucky enough to be on the Bay Bombers would skate in the Bay Area from late May until the first week in October, when the play-offs and championship matches at the Cow Palace began. Skaters could get regular jobs during the day and skate at night. Since I was a journeyman carpenter, I could go back to my old job at Golden Gate Drywall. In later years, I chose to work at the Roller Derby warehouse, constructing new tracks in addition to repairing the older tracks for our next road trip.

The skaters on other teams would have a few weeks off before the summer road trips began. Home games were in New York, Chicago, Cincinnati, and Portland. Unfortunately, many of these skaters had to rely completely on their derby incomes. For most of them, that meant returning home during the summer season, hoping to be hired again for the winter road trip. For those of us who were able to skate both seasons, we averaged 225 games per year. Unlike basketball or baseball players, who logged 160 games in a year; football players, who played twenty games per year; or hockey players, who enjoyed a leisurely ninety games a year, we were both used and abused.

Winter meant playing in Green Bay, Wisconsin; Traverse City, Michigan; or possibly Duluth, Minnesota, where one can walk a mile out on the frozen Great Lakes and not worry about falling through the ice. The harsh winters made me appreciate the great weather we enjoy in California. Some of my favorite northeastern places were Oshkosh, Wisconsin, where they are famous for cheese, Kalamazoo, Michigan. In Oshkosh, I had my dental bridge made, a broken nose set twice, and a cauliflower ear drained a couple of times. Don't ask me why I chose to have work done there; it just worked out that way.

Another favorite place was Buffalo, New York, home of the original buffalo wings. Just a across down the street from the Buffalo arena was a little café featuring buffalo wings. You could buy them by the bucket—small, medium, and large—and the wings were rated as one alarm, two alarm, three alarm, or, the hottest of them all, four alarm. I only tried that one once. Wow!

The history of hot wings started in the firehouse around the corner from this little café in Buffalo. Firemen routinely took turns cooking the evening meal for the other firemen. One of them took the chicken wings and created a wonderful hot sauce to complement the dish. It was a big hit. Before long, other fire stations were asking them for the secret recipe. The firemen got the idea that maybe they were on to something, so they opened a little restaurant to sell hot wings. It was a big hit.

Every time we were in town or even within twenty miles of Buffalo, we would send the ladies over to buy large buckets of wings and bring them back to our motel. Before long, other restaurants all over the United States were selling hot wings. I knew hot wings had made it when I saw them for sale in Maui, Hawaii. Now there are people making hot, spicy wings and calling them buffalo wings. However, only a few places today still comply with the original recipe. Additionally, when I find them, I order more than I should, along with a couple of cold beers, and I'm all set to enjoy a meal while reflecting about the modest start of buffalo wings.

A place Francine and I always enjoyed was Indianapolis, Indiana. A great fan there made us knitted throws using our team colors. When we skated for the Jolters, she knitted an aqua-and-brown one. When we were on the Chicago Pioneers, she gave us a throw in red, white, and blue. Even though we were on the New England Braves for only two months, she knitted yellow-and-green throws for us. She even painted a picture of Francine and me, in addition to sending us many cards and letters. What a great fan!

We enjoyed seeing the northern lights while skating in a small town in northern British Columbia. It was cool. At midnight, it was still light outside, not completely dark. We could see these strange flashes of light across the sky. We were skating in an old barn with an ice-hockey floor inside, so there were only a few bleacher seats; mostly, it was standing room only. The game started at nine thirty at night because there was a special showing at the movie house, and everyone in town voted for us to start our game after the movie was over. This was a small but savvy little town. The fans knew the game and the players, and they loved to yell.

St. Louis, Missouri, started building their landmark Gateway Arch in 1969 and finished it in 1972. We could see the beginnings of the arch from a hundred miles away—Missouri is really flat. I wish I had taken more pictures from the outside perimeters as we entered town from Omaha or Chicago, because it would have been great to knit them together to show how the arch grew out of the ground into the grand monument that it is today. We enjoyed Saint Louis and the fantastic fan support. We had fans giving us gifts before the game. Fans gave us all sorts of things, such as embroidered towels, dishes, plaques, and other handmade items. We enjoyed these testimonials to our skill in the sport and the following we had built.

West Virginia was an interesting place. It was poor, and the little buildings we skated in were barely large enough to hold our track, not to mention the people who would stand rather than sit in the bleachers available. I hired one young man, about nineteen years old, to sell programs. Most of the cities we played would take a 35 percent to 55 percent cut of sales as a fee for the building. This little town had no such fees. We could negotiate any price we wanted. I told the young man he would receive 25 percent, or twenty-five cents a program. He was happy with that arrangement. That night, he made almost $200, which was more than his dad made working in the coal mine for a month. The young man wanted to go on the road with us to sell programs. I explained that all the buildings had their own people to sell programs, so the likelihood of getting to sell programs was slim to none. However, he followed us to four games, sleeping in his car and trying each night to get hired again. Sadly, he finally gave up. It was hard not to help him, but the buildings had their own employees, and the managers were not open to hiring an outside person. I sometimes wonder what happened to that young man. He most likely grew up to become governor of West Virginia. It wouldn't surprise me in the least.

Another place that interested me was Atlanta, Georgia. Again, the fans were great, and they had a cornerman for the boxers who fought in the arena from time to time. I had chronic neck problems from my carpenter days, and this persistent problem had recently gotten much worse. One night, after getting the crap beat out of me, my teammates helped me to the dressing room to recover. The cornerman was cleaning up in another area as they carried me to a table in the middle of the dressing room. Moaning and groaning, I was holding my neck while trying to massage the pain away, when the cornerman came over and asked me what had happened. I explained the history of my neck pain, and he told me to take off my skates and socks. I thought, *Why should I take off my skates and socks, when my neck and head are hurting?* He briefly explained to me in a patient tone the concept of pressure points and the art of massaging the pressure points in my feet to provide relief to my neck.

Because I had taken some karate classes and understood pressure points and kick spots, this idea made sense to me. Within a few minutes, he pushed on spots in my feet and hands, and the pain disappeared. He showed me a few more pressure points for other aches as well. By the time he was done, other skaters had come in to check on me. I told them about the cornerman's treatment, but he had left the building. Even though we played many more games at that venue, I never saw the man again. However, I appreciated the lesson he taught me and bought a great book on the art of using pressure points, acupressure, and acupuncture. This was in 1969, and Chinese medicine was not in vogue at the time.

Camping was something Francine and I enjoyed. Cliff Butler and his wife and Mike and Judy McGuire often joined us. When we competed in Reno, Nevada, we often took advantage of the opportunity to camp at Sutter's Mill on the American River, where the 1849 gold rush started. Mike, Cliff, and I would scuba dive in the river, searching for gold. We ended up purchasing a sluice box to mine gold by hand. We fished in the river for our meals but often ended up buying steaks or chops for dinner.

One time, Francine and I traveled to Reno for an appearance on the Jerry Lewis telethon. We signed autographs, gave out books on the Roller Derby, and made pledges based on the number of tickets sold for our upcoming games. We took our tent and Coleman stove to the Reno campgrounds and enjoyed hiking and fishing for three days. Then, on the afternoon we were to appear on the show, we dressed up in our finest TV-appearance clothing. It was late July—100 degrees outside, with 20 percent humidity. It was hot. Francine had picked out a nice summer dress, and I wore a three-piece suit. I know—I wasn't thinking clearly. I was more concerned about the safety of our camping gear and food, and I picked up the wrong garment bag: the one containing a winter wool tweed suit. I was roasting by the time the master of ceremonies got around to us. I casually took off the coat during the interview while remarking about the heat. No one said anything about my relaxed attire, so I guess it all went well. We sold out that game.

Fisherman's Wharf in San Francisco was always a favorite place for us after a Sunday afternoon spent skating at Kezar Pavilion. We would finish our game, do the obligatory postgame interviews, and be ready for dinner at six o'clock. Francine and I would go to the wharf for fresh crab when it was in season or sometimes to Japantown for sushi. When Mike and Judy Gammons were in town, we went to Tokyo Sushiaki for traditional Japanese cuisine complete with shoji screen rooms, pillows on the floor, and tables that were eight inches high. The food was great, and the sake was smooth. Several times, we had so much fun that we had to stay over in the city instead of driving home.

The best place wasn't located where we skated; it was on the way to a game in Michigan. It was just a small town we passed through while driving from Atlanta. Anne Calvello had a toothache for several days and didn't visit a dentist to get it fixed. She was in bad shape. As we were driving a few miles outside of Atlanta, she honked her horn and flashed her lights to get my attention so that I would pull over. She was in great pain and wanted us to stop at the first dentist office we saw.

We were in a small southern town, and as we drove down the main street, we spotted a well-worn sign: Painless Dentist. It looked just like a dentist office in the movies. I walked with Anne up the stairs of this rickety old building into the dark office of a dentist claiming to be painless. Anne was hurting so bad that all she could do was tell him to pull the bad tooth and give her lots of Novocain. He had her in the dental chair and gave her a shot before extracting the bad tooth. I stood by, holding her hand while she tried not to scream. In a few minutes, the tooth was out, and the pain killers kicked in. I helped Anne to the backseat of her car, and one of the skaters riding with her took over driving duties. It was one of those times in life when you needed to be there in order to fully appreciate the scene.

That story reminds me of a time when Francine, being new to the United States, had never eaten tacos or any Mexican food and wanted me to cook some for her. I was more than willing since I loved Mexican food, especially tacos. My mother had taught me how to cook tacos, and they were great. I used corn tortillas; fresh ground beef; fresh lettuce, tomatoes, and onions; and hot sauce. I'm proud to say that I love to cook, and my tacos are great. There was only one problem: kids in Montreal and the French Canadian families in particular do not have good teeth. It has something to do with the water and poor dental hygiene. Francine had a decayed front tooth and was sensitive about how it affected her appearance.

I prepared the tacos and invited our next-door neighbors, Gladys and Charlie, over to share them with us. After Francine took one bite of her taco, her front tooth broke off. This was a Saturday afternoon, and we had a game later that night at the Oakland Coliseum.

Poor Francine had to wait until Monday to see a dentist. Our apartment was near a dentist's office, so we walked to the office for treatment. The dentist took some x-rays and decided to pull the bad tooth. While doing the exam, he determined that Francine needed $2,500 in major dental work. In 1968, that was a lot of money—the equivalent of $20,000 today. But the work needed to be done, and over the next four to five weeks, Francine got her dental work done. She has a wonderful smile, so the work was worth the sacrifice.

My next story centers on my coach, Bert, and his attempt to seduce one of our female skaters while we were skating in Chicago. Bert was married to a beautiful woman who stayed in California while Bert went on the road. Bert had a reputation as a bad boy. He wanted to seduce our teammate and heard that she liked the beach, the ocean, and tropical atmospheres. So Bert went down to a lumberyard to get bags of sand. Then he took the sheet off his hotel bed and spread out the sand to form a beach affect. He found a plastic palm tree and some shells to decorate his tropical beach bed. It looked good. Subsequently, Bert took her out for an expensive dinner and drinks—a lot of drinks.

They returned to Bert's room, where he would spring the trap. The instant she saw what was going on, she started laughing—I mean really laughing. Bert thought this was a great sign. As he started to make his move, she told him she was a lesbian. Needless to say, Bert didn't get any beach time that night. He did get a bill from the hotel for removal of all that sand. I sometimes wonder what happened to the palm tree and shells.

Another Bert story isn't about Bert himself but about his 1961 Chevrolet Corvair, which I often drove when Bert flew to another city. If you recall the history of this infamous little four-passenger sports car, you remember that it had bad brake problems and an engine that had a habit of catching fire. The trip I remember most was a trip from Chicago to Southern California. Jo Jo Stafford, two other skaters, and I were crammed into this mousetrap, along with most of our luggage. We had to load some of our stuff onto the truck with our track. Bert boarded a plane for California the morning after we dismantled the track in Chicago and headed west by road. The trip was uneventful, except the guys traveling with me pulled an eat-and-run. We stopped at a little restaurant in some small town for dinner. After dinner, I left money to cover my bill and the tip before going to the restroom. When I came out, my three passengers headed for the car. I assumed they had paid for their meals. As soon as we got to the car, the guys were anxious for me to get in and get going. I asked why they were all in such a hurry, and they told me that there were a couple of Klansmen in the restaurant, so they wanted out of there quickly. Just as I pulled away, I noticed the waiter and two other guys bolting out of the restaurant door. They were heading straight toward our car. I backed up, shifted gears, and tore out of the parking lot, leaving a little rubber as I went.

The guys from the restaurant didn't follow us, but we kept up our speed, getting out of the area as quickly as possible. In those days, in that state, when one entered an interstate highway, the speed-limit sign posted was Resume Safe Speed. In our case, that meant at least ninety miles per hour. I didn't learn the real reason the guys wanted to leave as quickly as possible until the next time we stopped to eat. They wanted to try another eat-and-run, but I refused to join in. As you might have guessed, an eat-and-run is when one orders food, eats it, and then sneaks out without paying the bill. Normally, a couple of guys would go to the restroom and then quietly slip out to the car without paying while the others at the table pretended to be walking to the restroom. They would sneak out a side door to a waiting car before speeding off. I was taught not to cheat, steal, or lie, so I refused to play the game, which pissed off my traveling companions.

The next incident with the Corvair happened as we were driving across the Mojave Desert. We ran into a sandstorm so bad that at one point, we had to pull off to the side of the road. The wind was blowing so hard that I could barely keep the car on the pavement. Visibility was so poor that it was unsafe to continue. I noticed cars ahead of me pulling off the road, and the oncoming traffic was also stopping. The wind finally abated about twenty minutes later. During the storm, we could hardly breathe inside the car, with sand coming in through the cracks in the windows and the convertible top. This car was not sealed well, and we were all coughing and wondering if this was the end. As soon as the wind died down a little, I started the car and began to move back onto the highway. That was when I realized that my half of the windshield and side window had been sandblasted, pitting the glass. I could barely see to drive. I was forced to position myself toward the center console while shifting gears and trying to depress the clutch. We only had about three more hours of driving before we arrived at Bert's home, but the first order of business was to drop off the other skaters at the Greyhound bus terminal so that they could get safely back to the Bay Area.

When I got to Bert's home, he came out and immediately asked what had happened to the windshield. I recounted the events surrounding the sandstorm and how we had nearly died in the blowing sand. Bert said he understood. I asked him when my flight to the Bay Area departed. To my surprise, he said we would be driving to the Bay Area using his other car and would be leaving for home right away. I was tired and hadn't slept for almost forty-eight hours. I was shot. We packed my stuff into Bert's Mercedes with the help of his wife. They said their good-byes, and we hit the road. She had packed sandwiches and some sodas in an ice chest for the trip. I was starving and quickly downed a sandwich and soda, and then I climbed into the backseat and slept the entire seven-hour trip back to my home in Oakland, California.

Bert sold the Corvair before our next road trip. On that trip, I drove Jerry Seltzer's 1965 El Camino pickup with Don Drewry and Ken Kunzelman along for companionship. A few months after Bert sold the Corvair, we heard the reports of bad brakes and engine fires.

ROBERT "BOBBY" SEEVER

I received an e-mail from Bobby's daughter, Marla, informing me of his passing on the morning of Tuesday, December 18, 2007. They had a memorial on January 12. God rest his soul.

Sharing the same sense of humor, Bobby and I had lots of fun on the road. He was one of our truck drivers as well as a referee. Bobby was a skater for several years before I started skating; however, I got to skate against him a couple of times. He was fast and hit like a bulldozer. He loved to pull practical jokes, and when he was around, we had to check our skate bags for snakes, spiders, dead rats, and so on.

He had a sinister side as well. He was always on the edge of wrongdoings. I remember telling him several times, "Bobby, you are going to go to jail." He finally did. When I met his wife at a reunion in 2006, she told me he was in prison.

Bobby, your secrets are safe with me. May God have mercy on your soul.

OH NO! TWO DAYS OFF
IN RHODE ISLAND

In 1964 or 1965, it had been a while since my first visit to Rhode Island and my first Roller Derby venue, when I found myself there with two days off after a grueling trip on the road. I knew we were all ready to relax and blow off some steam. I didn't understand why the road trips always meant sixteen to seventeen days straight without a day off, including our long drives to the next city. The facts were clear for seasoned agents who had lived through rest periods in cities as boring as where the Rhode Island Reds played. However, in those days, it was a boring place to be in February.

We had been on the road since the first week in January, and we'd had few days off, when we arrived at a nice, private hotel in Rhode Island. Everyone arrived late one evening and slept in the following morning. By early afternoon, everyone was drifting into the only restaurant, a diner across from the hotel, to enjoy lunch and the best Boston cream pie I had ever eaten. It was incredible. At about five o'clock, we talked about going to a bar for some drinks since we had the next day off. I had to bow out because of my upcoming court appearance for being underage in a bar in Chicago a few days before, so a couple of other nondrinkers and I headed for the movie theater.

When we returned to the hotel, all was quiet—too quiet. Almost all the other skaters were at a bar, blowing off steam while fending off truckers. I never understood why they always seemed to head straight to a truckers' bar. It might have been because they loved to get into fistfights. However, they got paid to fight on the track, so why would they want to fight and possibly go to jail?

At about two o'clock in the morning, the noise level rose substantially. Everyone came back to the hotel and began singing, yelling, and talking loudly. Before long, pranks started, and someone shoved a piece of that fine-tasting Boston cream pie into the face of an unsuspecting victim. Then came the shaving-cream fights, followed by whipped-cream fights. The next afternoon, the melee evolved into water-balloon fights. I learned firsthand about short-sheeting with whipped cream added into the folds of the bedsheets. What a mess!

The hotel manager was called in to stop the mayhem when the fights involved the use of fire hoses. The manager was appropriately creamed, watered, and pelted as he did his best to stop the derby group from ruining his hotel. Fortunately, it was a small hotel, and there were few other guests. Those with a sense of humor joined in, and others simply stayed in their rooms to avoid the confrontation. After a few calls back and forth between the left and right coast, Jerry Seltzer struck a bargain, and everyone calmed down.

By game day, things were back to normal, and I went with the crew to set up the track. I was told to take my baggage with me since we had been thrown out of the hotel and told to never to come back. Imagine that!

A few years later, we returned to that hotel and found that it had changed hands. The new owners had added a nice family restaurant and a small bar with a TV, so we could watch Monday Night Football, the new rage for Monday nights. The rooms were nicely decorated. This time, we enjoyed our night off with few riotous incidents. Being occupied with the Monday-night game must have helped. The Oakland Raiders kicked butt that night.

The only incident was a short-sheeting involving Tony "the Tuna" D'Nofrio. He was flattered that he had been short-sheeted. He felt it meant the team had accepted him. Of course, he was right. Unfortunately, the next morning, Francine and I had to drive him to the airport so that he could return to California—he'd received word that his father had passed on.

ON-THE-ROAD CATTLE CALLS

Around 1968 or 1969, the Roller Derby was doing great—so great that we were running out of skaters. The only training center, located at 105th Avenue in Oakland, California, managed by George Kadounas, could not keep up with the demand, even though he had a lot of trainees. The problem, you see, was the pay scale, as well as the road-trip commitments. Skaters had to commit to a five-month road-trip schedule that involved working as many as seventeen days straight, living in Holiday Inns, making five-hundred- to seven-hundred-mile trips every night, and rooming with three or four skaters. Oh, and did I mention the pay scale then was sixty-five dollars a week with a fifteen-dollar-a-week food allowance?

If one really loved the game, he or she would sacrifice everything to do it. We had married couples with children leave their families to join the Roller Derby. Many skaters would quit after only a few weeks, while others were sent home with injuries. It didn't take long for rookies to flee. Replacements were needed, so Jerry Seltzer and Hal Janowitz called me in to handle the so-called cattle calls. We would set up in some of the large cities, such as Chicago, Omaha, and Cincinnati. As with actors and dancers, cattle calls went out over the television waves, announcing that there would be tryouts for skater positions the following Saturday morning in their town. Fame and fortune awaited them if they were good enough, the ads promised.

The first time I managed the tryouts was in Chicago at the old coliseum once used as a Civil War prison. Yes, it was that old. I expected maybe twenty to fifty recruits to show up, but instead, more than two hundred starry-eyed hopefuls waiting for their shot at stardom confronted me. When I saw all of those kids beginning to register, I almost panicked. How could I handle that many hopefuls without killing their dreams and still discover the four skaters we needed? I had to find two men and two women who were willing to travel and hopefully could skate. The traveling requirement was more important than their skating ability. Of course, I didn't let them know that.

During those days, I was working on the track crew as well as skating, so I arrived at the coliseum early to help set up. I knew I was in over my head, so I asked Dave Cannella and Bill Morrissey to hang around afterward to help me coordinate the new skaters by getting them registered and numbered. I started with ten men and then ten women, alternating them as they were put through their paces for five to seven minutes. I showed them the basic five-stride pacing and how to use the track in addition to centrifugal force to make their way smoothly and quickly around the track. If they could do this with a little instruction, I told them to take a seat and wait until we started the next phase of the tryout. Normally, I would take one man and one woman for the next phase. This might not have been the best way to sort them out, but time was limited.

During the registration portion, Dave and Bill explained the road trips, including the hard conditions, the number of consecutive workdays required, and the travel from town to town in cars packed with three or four skaters, not to mention stays at hotels with several skaters crammed into a room. In those days, hotels typically had two double or queen-sized beds. The first two skaters took the mattresses off the box springs and made four beds. The first skaters to arrive had mattresses, while the late comers had to make do with the remaining box springs. It was either that or sleeping together, which most of us didn't care to do.

After qualifying the first cadre of skaters, I started the next phase of ten women and ten men. By this time, I had them skating at higher speeds, and I required them to deliberately take falls on the straightaway and then get back up and run on their skates to the next turn, only to fall again on the next straightaway. I provided them with instructions as well as a demonstration on how to fall with their hands up in the air. I didn't want any broken hands, wrists, or arms. However, a few bruised bottoms were necessary for this process. Using the same process of elimination, I narrowed the group down for phase three.

In phase three, I demonstrated how to take a block without falling—in most cases, taking a block, falling down, and then returning to the pack as soon as possible. This eliminated the wannabes from the "I can take it!" folks quickly. I knew the type of person who could and would last in a real Roller Derby game.

In 1967, after receiving a concussion and a broken nose, I was sent home for surgery. During the healing process, I was sent to Montreal to open a training school with the goal of developing two new teams. I wanted skaters who were hungry for the game and stardom. Those kids would fall while practically killing themselves to get up and run on their skates. They would build up speed till they were back in the pack, and then they would do it all over again. Those were the kids I wanted.

The last phase finally arrived, and there were about thirty men and twenty women left who had survived the first three phases. In groups of ten at a time, I divided them into teams to skate minigames against each other. They loved the opportunity to actually skate a real Roller Derby game on a real Roller Derby track. Those who hadn't made the cut stayed to watch. It didn't take long for us to find our new players.

Unfortunately, of the first group, all were eliminated before the end of the road trip due to injuries, bruised egos, or home sickness. However, we would find more recruits in Cincinnati.

OPENING IN LITTLE ROCK, ARKANSAS

In 1968, we were rockin' and a-rollin'. Every venue was a sellout with standing room only. We had divided the San Francisco Bay Area Bombers into two traveling road teams in order to meet the increased demand. Charlie O'Connell headed to the San Francisco Bombers, while Joanie Weston went to the Oakland Bay Area Bombers. Francine and I were with Joanie and Ken Monte, our coach. We were having a ball, skating an average of sixteen days straight before we got a day off. Usually, that meant a thousand-mile trip before we could rest.

Anyway, the point of this story is the opening of a new arena in Little Rock, Arkansas. It wasn't the opening that was special, because we were doing openings a lot. This incident was notable because that region of the country was extremely prejudiced back in 1968. We were playing the New York Chiefs with Big, Bad Bob Woodbury, who was black. Well, Bob was knocking the crap out of me on every jam. In those days, Mike Gammon and I alternated jammer and then blocker after each play. We skated every jam, either as the jammer or a blocker. The announcers told the crowd that my mother was from Arkansas, which was true. My birth mother was from Arkansas; however, I hadn't seen her since I was five years old. But the fans loved me for it and hated Big, Bad Bob. I thought they were going to riot and hustle Bob out for a neck stretching. I was worried.

Bob had a bad habit of kicking backward into my groin when he blocked me, and it hurt. Additionally, he would grab me in a head lock and punch me in the nose; again, that did not feel good. On one play, just before halftime, Bob kicked me in the groin and followed up the kick with a headlock and a punch in the nose. I had had enough. When I got back up, I was half a lap behind the pack, and I was mad as hell. Adrenaline was rushing through me when I got up, and I cut through the infield as fast as I could and caught Bob as he was coming toward me. I dropped my right fist so low that it was touching the track as I drove an upper cut right to Bob's chin, knocking him down. Then I stood over him, daring him to get up.

The referees rushed over, and play stopped. The fans were in a frenzy, jumping up and down. Bob was sitting on the track with a bloody lip and a dazed look on his face. His trainer helped him to the infield and into a chair. The crowd was so loud that I thought the roof might come off. It was nearly halftime, and Bob's trainer helped him to the dressing room. This made the crowd cheer even more. I think that upper cut might have saved Bob's life. At least it probably saved him from being lynched by the KKK.

In the dressing room, Bob was lying on a table, resting, so I skated up to him and asked how he was doing. He asked if I was mad at him, since I had never retaliated like that before. I told him the truth: I was mad, but now I felt better. We shook hands, and deep down, I was full of satisfaction. Even though I had a couple of broken knuckles along with a sprained wrist, it was worth it.

PAINTSVILLE, KENTUCKY, AND MY 1967 GTO

In early 1967, while touring cities in the Great Smoky Mountains, we were traveling to Memphis, Tennessee, from God knows where, on an early morning with light fog and icy roadways. We were forced to take back roads. Normally, I didn't caravan, but J. J. Burton, Pete Boyd, Jo Jo Stafford, and others had asked if they could follow me. Because of the poor road conditions and weather, I'd agreed.

We were up before dawn, having breakfast at a Denny's restaurant. By the time we climbed into our cars for the five-hundred-mile trip, the sun was shining brightly. The temperature hovered in the high twenties, and the two-lane road was littered with dangerous patches of ice. I was driving my pride and joy, an ocean-blue 321 CI 1967 GTO. My wife, Francine Cochu, was in the bucket seat next to me, and Jackie Garillo occupied the backseat. We had only traveled for about an hour, when, suddenly, coming around a turn, I saw a tow truck straddling both lanes. His hitch was connected to a car on the right side of the roadway, and to the left side was a large tree with an old car parked nearby. Along the left side, a river ran parallel to the roadway, with a foot bridge running across to a farmhouse. In back of me, too close to my tail, J. J. Burton was driving her full-size Pontiac Bonneville with the other skaters inside.

If you have ever been in an accident, you understand how I perceived all of these things in a flash and had to make a split-second decision: Should I slam on my brakes and hit the tow truck and car, knowing that the truck driver, standing at the winch, would probably not survive? Or should I try to hit the tree and the parked wrecked car between me and the river? My only other option would have been to plunge into the river, not knowing how deep the water was. What would you have done? I hit the wrecked car and part of the tree, almost ending up in the river. The front end of my car snagged a tree root, while the back end stuck up into the sky.

As soon as our car stopped, Jackie Garillo and I started yelling at Francine to get out before the car flipped over into the river. I was holding my foot on the brake, thinking that would stop the car from flipping over. I didn't know until we were safely out of the car that it was snagged on the tree root.

While all of this was going on, I caught a glimpse of J. J.'s car going into the river just before we hit the car and tree. I looked over and saw that her car was upside down in the water. My first thought was that they were drowning in the river. As soon as Francine and Jackie were out of the car, I rushed to the river's edge while taking off my jacket and shoes for a plunge into the water to rescue J. J. and her passengers. Just as I arrived, I saw that they all had made it safely to the river bank. Thank God!

By the time I learned that no one was hurt, the trucker and the driver of the stranded car were at my side, asking if everyone was okay. About then, J. J. started yelling, "Oh! My baby! Please get my baby out! Oh my God!" Of course, I knew who—or, more accurately, what—her baby was. I dove into the water and pulled her tiny, soaking-wet miniature poodle from the car. Needless to say, the tow-truck driver was ready to kill. The other driver wasn't showing much sympathy either. While all of this was going on, the owner of the wrecked car by the tree was running across the foot bridge, yelling about her poor car. She said nothing about the other wrecked cars or the occupants. We later learned that her car had been hit four other times in the last few months, and each time, she received insurance money for the repairs, which had never been performed. Additionally, the roadway was icy going into the turn, and I suspect she'd used the garden hose left near her car to create the hazard by spraying water on the turn and then letting nature take its course. Too bad I couldn't prove it.

Please keep in mind that this was 1967 in Kentucky, and J. J. and her three other passengers were African Americans. With all of us stranded and needing to get to Memphis for the next game, we decided we could be towed into Paintsville, where there was body shop, a car rental, and a motel. J. J. and I would stay at the motel until they got my car repaired—a two-day job. J. J.'s insurance company considered the car totaled. She would need to purchase another car in Memphis.

This town only had one motel, and the owners normally didn't allow blacks to stay there. But since she was a Roller Derby star, they agreed to give us two adjoining rooms. Even so, J. J. wanted to have some degree of protection. I often wonder how I could have protected her if the KKK had shown up. Fortunately, that didn't happen, but we did have moonshiners knock on our doors and ask if we wanted to buy any 'shine. We both bought a mason jar full of homemade white whiskey. It came in real handy.

After two days, my car was ready to go. J. J. and I drove into the next city after Memphis to reunite with our teams and friends. J. J. had to find a replacement for her totaled car. I drove my damaged GTO for another three months before I could get back to the Bay Area to have the car properly repaired. I sold it shortly after. I miss that car, but I will always remember moonshine in Paintsville.

ANN CALVELLO

There are many stories I could tell about Ann Calvello. She was a classy lady in her time. I believe she started skating competitively in the 1950s and retired in the early 1980s. She was known for her wild-colored hair—anything from white with patriotic stars to red with blonde flames and everything in between. Additionally, she always had a California tan, usually maintained by using the heat lamps in Holiday Inn bathrooms.

In 1971, I had the great pleasure of working with Annie on the Ohio Jolters with Cliff Butler as coach. Annie was the girls' team captain, while I served as men's captain. Our home base was in Cincinnati, and we roomed in the Quality Courts Hotel, a nice place for us. Annie had an ongoing relationship with the young hotel manager. Annie liked her men young. We got whatever we wanted because of Annie. But we were careful not to abuse our privileges. We did ask him to take her out to dinner for her birthday while the whole team went through a hair-color change to surprise her. Francine had been a beautician as a teenager before I charmed her away from her Montreal home. She had learned the hair-dying secret that allowed Annie to change the color of her hair every night if she chose to. The secret was food coloring instead of hair dye. After washing your hair and drying it until it was slightly damp, you sprayed the base food coloring on your hair and then used cutouts, such as stars, half moons, and stripes, to spray a variety of colorful patterns—whatever your theme for the night called for.

When Annie and her date returned from dinner, he asked Annie to go along on a check of the banquet rooms before heading to the bar. The whole team was waiting for her to enter the room, with our hair done in numerous colors, shapes, and styles. We all sang "Happy Birthday" to her. I had never seen her cry before, but she did while screaming, shouting, laughing, and just having a great time. We celebrated with a delicious cake prepared by the hotel dining staff and lots of champagne and dancing. I miss her friendship.

Some of the other stories worth reflecting on are her LOVER California license plates, her silver chalice, and her total domination of any bar she found herself in, not to mention one of my personal favorites: the painless dentist.

During the late 1960s, California led the nation with personalized license plates, but in other states, traffic-enforcement officers were not aware of this. They constantly pulled Annie over for no other reason than her LOVER license plates. Now, try to imagine: it was four o'clock in the morning in Podunk, Nebraska, when a state trooper saw a white Lincoln from California with plates that read LOVER. Usually, since it was so early in the morning, Annie or her driver, usually a young male rookie, would be driving too fast. The troopers would pull the car over, and either Annie would be driving with that wild-colored hair with stripes, stars, or worse, or her young chauffer would be at the wheel, and Annie would pop up from the backseat, looking like the Wicked Witch of the West. Knowing Annie, she would yell at the cops for waking her up. Once they realized who she was, they often wanted to take pictures for the wife and kids back home, which made Annie more incensed. However, if would help get her out of a ticket, she would graciously allow them to take photos after she primped a bit. If the troopers were young and good looking, she would arrange for them to get tickets for the next game in their area.

When Annie went to a bar, she took it over. It didn't matter if it was full of biker dudes, truckers, or gays, she could dominate three conversations at once. She would be yelling out rules of conduct for the other players in the room or to loudmouths who tried to top her. She always had a pithy comeback. The other trait that made her queen of the bar was the silver chalice she placed on the bar as her drinking goblet with instructions to keep it full. Happy Roller Derby fans always kept it full as she cursed and yelled at them while telling the dirtiest jokes in the bar. Annie Calvello was always queen of the bar.

I know I have told this story before, but it is worth repeating, and I'm sure Anne would agree. One of the funniest times with Annie was a trip from Cincinnati to somewhere in Michigan on our day off. Annie had a terrible toothache, and we had a long drive before we could stop to get some sleep. We were wagon-training it with six cars in a caravan through the South before heading north. Before getting on the interstate highway, we had to find a dentist for Annie. One of the little towns we came to first had a second-story dentist's office with a hand-painted sign that read Painless Dentist on the outside of an old wooden building that had seen better days. Annie insisted on stopping to see if the dentist was in. Fortunately for her, he was. At least ninety years old, he was as skinny as a rail and as loud as Annie. He talked her into letting him pull the bad tooth out while, of course, giving her some of the finest pain-killing drugs money could buy. After a couple of drinks in the saloon below the office, we were on our way to Michigan. Annie slept almost the whole way, for seventeen hours straight. We were beginning to worry about her. We arrived just in time to suit up and skate. Annie was a trooper. She had one of her best nights skating.

We all miss Annie Calvello. She died in 2006 in San Francisco. She had been working as a grocery bagger in a local supermarket there. She was unmarried.

BOB WOODBERRY'S THREE-DAY CONSTRUCTION LIFE

Big, Bad Bob Woodberry of the New York Chiefs and the Red Devils was built like a lean heavyweight fighter without an ounce of fat or loose skin. He was strong, fast, and agile but not the sharpest knife in the drawer, if you know what I mean. I have written other short tales of Bob's exploits and skating antics, but this is one of his life lessons that I have held back until now.

Bob was short on money, so he decided to use his star power to knock off one of the less-known skaters from the track crew. Keep in mind that the starting salary for a rookie skater was sixty-five dollars a week, plus a fifteen-dollar food allowance and all the Masonite he or she could eat.

If one was lucky enough to work on the track crew, he or she could make an additional $125 per week setting up and tearing down the derby track—not bad in those days. It meant the difference between eating bologna sandwiches all week and feasting on Kentucky Fried Chicken, hamburgers, and a beer now and then. So when Bob had a skater taken off the crew so that he could take the job, it made us all mad. Bob was making more than $200 per week as a skater.

The first day Bob worked the track crew, he showed up late—not a good start. Additionally, he wasn't a good worker. He loved to talk more than work. We were getting a guaranteed five hours for setup and three hours for teardown. If we all busted our butts, we could set up in one to one and a half hours and tear down in forty-five minutes to one hour and fifteen minutes. After the game, Bob was the last crew member out of the dressing room to help. He would have a couple of beers first and then head out to work. Before joining the Roller Derby, I had worked as a carpenter with people who had poor work habits. In fact, I'd joined the Carpenter's Union as an eighteen-year-old journeyman—something not normally done. My great-grandfather, grandfather, and dad, as well as two uncles, were all carpenters. They had been training me since I was twelve years old.

Bob was assigned a job as a runner, taking the pieces of track on a stage and carting them out of the building to the truck and then up a twenty-foot ramp into the truck, where I would help move the two-hundred-pound pieces of track into place and lock them into position. This job required two men in the truck, plus the runner bringing in the track sections. The sections were made with dexi steel sides that allowed them to be bolted to other pieces of track. The dexi steel made it easy to slide and move the pieces on edge and into position. I had an idea that I knew was wrong, but I didn't like what Bob had done by removing one of the kids from the crew who needed the money to survive on the road with us.

When Bob brought in a four-by-twelve-foot piece of track, I would stand on the edge of the dexi and let Bob do all the pushing while I rode the rail. When we were setting up the track, we did the process in reverse, so I would ride the rail again while Bob did the work of pulling the track section out to the rear doorway of the truck. It only took three days for Bob to cry uncle, retiring from the track crew and subsequently relinquishing his position to the rookie. Bob, when you read this, I hope you'll get a big laugh out of it and let me buy you a few beers—maybe several.

CHARLOTTE MOTOR SPEEDWAY

In 1968, our road-trip manager and promoter for the South was a fine gentleman named William Campbell; he was a true businessman and hardworking promoter. He also had a love for fast cars. Doubling his duties with booking the Roller Derby, Bill also booked races for the Charlotte Motor Speedway. We were fortunate to have a couple of days off in Charlotte, North Carolina. Bill arranged for us to ride in the official pace car, screaming around the racetrack at 120 miles per hour. What a thrill!

The car took two of us at a time, and we were buckled in for a four-lap, hug-the-wall ride so that we could really feel the g-forces as the car accelerated around the track. Mike Gammon, Don Drewry, Ken Kunzelman, Candy Jones, Lydia Clay, Caroline Moreland, and I were the lucky riders.

The night before, Mike and Judy Gammon, Don Drewry, Francine, and I went across the street from our hotel to a nice little Italian restaurant. Among the five of us, we had sixteen bottles of Chianti. Yes, sixteen bottles! Needless to say, Judy and Francine were not up to taking the ride the next morning. As a matter of fact, two days later, Francine fell during warm-ups and was accused of tripping on some grapes. However, Francine did not drink and had only been a spectator during the consumption of the Chianti.

After taking us around the track and giving us the thrill of a lifetime, Bill challenged us to walk up the asphalt turn on all fours. We weren't allowed to stand up and walk like a normal person. The challenge gave us a sense of the dynamics, centrifugal force, and speed. A few weeks later, Bill took us into one of the shops where the cars were built. It was another fun day. We saw how mechanics precisely measured engines, received twenty at a time, with micrometers to find the perfect engine parts so that they could build factory engines and still run stock. Additionally, we saw how they built the frame and body as well as all the safety items necessary to create a winning stock car. I will always remember the speed trials and the shop tour. I have great respect for the racers, builders, and mechanics of any racing endeavor.

CINCINNATI GARDENS

I just returned from Middletown, Ohio. While there, I visited the Cincinnati Gardens, where we skated Jolter home games from January 1971 through May 1973. The arena was closed, except for the ticket office, which was open to sell tickets for ice hockey. Diane Sass, my special person, and I went in and walked around the arena. It felt different after thirty-four years. One of the building managers walked up to us and asked if we needed anything. I told him why we were there. He, in turn, offered a trip through fifty years of history at the Garden Events Museum. Of course we agreed to walk with him down memory lane. The museum was a large room set aside for artifacts, posters, pictures, uniforms, and other memorabilia. The cases were about one hundred feet long and twenty feet high. There was one section for Roller Derby, including posters, pictures of the 1973 Jolters, and the front pages from the Chicago Pioneers historic old programs. I promised to send him a picture of the 1973 Jolters to add to the collection once we returned home.

We'd planned our trip to Ohio to celebrate Diane's uncle Stan's eighty-ninth birthday and to have a meet and greet with Diane's family. Unfortunately, the afternoon before we left, we learned that her uncle's only son, Dick, had suddenly died at the age of fifty-two from a heart attack. The happy trip we'd expected turned into a mournful one for all. The trip was consumed with funeral plans and tearful reunions. Dick was buried the next morning in Ohio.

Today I received an e-mail telling me of the death of Jo Jo Stafford, number 7 of the Ohio Jolters. He fought cancer for several months before finally losing the battle. Jo Jo was a good man and a great skater. He was lean and as feisty as they come. I found out that Jo Jo was involved with the Junior Olympics as a way to help his son become a better athlete. I pray that Jo Jo is managing God's track team in heaven.

Jo Jo, I hope you know how much your fellow skaters loved you. I will always remember you as one of the best players and speedsters on the track.

ANDRE DEEK

Andre Deek, a former soccer player from Hungary, moved to the United States on a temporary visa and then applied for a position as a trainer in the Roller Derby. He worked with us for seven years, tending to our wounds, scrapes, and sore muscles. He knew a lot about medicine and sports care. Apparently, he was studying to be a doctor when the soccer bug hit him. He dropped out of school to play soccer on the Hungarian National Soccer Team.

He was good looking, well mannered, and physically fit, and he loved the company of women. Andre had a different woman in his room nearly every night. He spent most of his infield time during the game making eyes at the ladies and then getting their names and phone numbers, hoping for a little romance after the game. Don't get me wrong; Andre took good care of us before and during the game. However, after the game, he would set up his romantic encounters and still help us tear down the track.

His father was still living in Hungary, which was a Communist state at that time. Andre was prohibited from returning, even though his father was a judge. He would sometimes share his frustration with the government and sincerely tried to get his dad to join him in the United States. But sadly, he failed to convince his father to immigrate. In the early 1970s, Andre was finally able to return to his homeland. He shipped two Ford Mustangs with him that he'd purchased here for resale once he finished driving them. In Hungary, Mustangs would sell for almost three times what they cost in the United States. Andre knew how to survive.

Many times, as we were unloading the track, Andre would try to juggle a soccer ball on his head, knees, and chest while working the unloading. Since we always had curious stagehands watching us unload, Andre had an audience and the opportunity to make a little extra money by hustling the locals. He would let the ball drop after a couple of minutes of juggling, and then he would get someone to bet him that he couldn't keep it going for two minutes. Naturally, after Andre lost the bet, he would boast that even though he might have dropped the ball, he could do it for three minutes. If one of the stagehands got into the bet, he would drop the ball after maybe two and a half minutes. He then would increase the bet, suckering the unsuspecting local into betting that he couldn't do it for five minutes. If you know hustling, you know that the outcome was always the same: Andre would win the bet. During our days off, he would practice juggling the soccer ball, and his best time was more than thirty minutes, at which point he got bored and let the ball fall.

Since Andre was such a great-looking guy, Ronnie "Sugar Ray's Kid" Robinson, who was a little light in the loafers, would often ask Andre to give him a massage with Bengay to warm up his muscles before a game. Normally, Andre wouldn't have any problems with Ronnie, but sometimes when Andre was telling or listening to a story intently, Ronnie would push his hand down where it didn't belong, and Andre would start cussing and yelling at him. Then Ronnie would almost fall off the table laughing. We all laughed. Several days would pass before Ronnie could persuade Andre to massage him again. Then the cycle would repeat.

Late in 1968, John Early joined us on the road. He shared a room with Andre. At that time, John was not a cool guy in his manners or his dress. He had difficulty enticing a woman into his room. But with Andre as a teacher, John quickly started dressing better and became cool in his talk and manners. Before long, he and Andre always seemed to have the best-looking women on their arms—although we thought John might have had to pay for their company occasionally.

Before the Roller Derby closed in 1973, Andre had already moved back to Hungary. A few years later, I heard that he had moved to New York after the death of his father. Andre never talked about other family members, and we suspected they might have disappeared as a result of the Communist state, considering the way Communists handled the people who opposed them.

BLOWOUT AT EIGHTY MILES PER HOUR

In 1967, Francine and I were touring on the road as usual, but this time, I was driving James Pierce's Lincoln Continental. Jim was one of our truck drivers and referees. Normally, I would have been driving my own car, getting gas money for my effort. However, since we had only been married for a couple of months, I was working at a gas station for peanuts. Selling my old car was the best alternative. While Jim got the gas money, I enjoyed the freedom of having a nice car on the road.

We were traveling through the Southwest, and it was early morning. I was driving between eighty and eighty-five miles per hour in light traffic in a state that had Resume Safe Speed speed-limit signs after city boundaries. Really, there was no posted speed limit at that time, just an admonishment to drive safely. Fortunately, I had extensive driving experience since my family had moved so often when I was growing up. I had experienced blowouts while driving but never while I was traveling more than eighty miles per hour. Francine was awake, while the two other skaters riding with us were asleep in the backseat. Suddenly, the right front tire blew out, and immediately, the car began to swerve to the right-hand side of the road toward a drainage ditch. I remembered not to hit the brakes but to gently turn the wheel away from the ditch and toward the roadway. We were lucky there was no oncoming traffic at that time. My car fishtailed a couple of times, but I was able to correct the slide while slowing down. I was fortunate to find a spot along the shoulder of the roadway wide enough to stop safely.

By the time the car came to a stop, the skaters in the back were wide awake, shouting that they were going to die. Francine was fairly calm, except she grabbed my leg near my thigh, unknowingly digging her fingernails into my skin. Ouch! Once the car had stopped, I climbed out to get a good look at the tire. It was gone! There was only a little bit of rubber still clinging to the rim. As I surveyed the landscape, I could see the outline of a gas station down the road. I decided to put on the spare and drive slowly on the shoulder to the gas station. I purchased a new tire, and the bad one was removed. It's a good thing the gas station was so close, since the spare tire wasn't in good condition.

It is surprising how aware you can become of your driving and the traffic around you given the condition of your tires, belts, and hoses. After all, I had worked at a gas station on and off for a couple of years, always looking for safety problems in the cars that came in for gas. The gas station I worked at paid a commission on tires, wipers, and batteries, so I was constantly on the lookout for worn parts and dangerous conditions. After that incident, I started doing safety checks on my car routinely. The experience allowed me to help some of the ladies perform safety checks on their cars as well.

We were lucky. God was there to keep us safe.

DAVE CANNELLA
LOSES A FINGER

Just when you think you have seen everything, life throws you a curve. So it was for Dave Cannella, our referee and truck driver. Dave was a great guy. He and I shared a room together off and on for the first couple of years on the road. I have many stories about Dave, but I'll concentrate on this one for now.

Often, Dave and I would work on the track after the initial setup, performing repairs, adjusting braces, moving Masonite, and painting to keep the track looking sharp for the game. The work day started out normally enough; Dave and I were inspecting the track, checking for lose bolts and screws. We were laughing and telling stories, some of which were true. The track setup had been completed early in the morning, so we had plenty of time to check things out.

Skaters were warned not to wear any type of jewelry, rings, or chains, because they might get caught on a screw or bolt and cause an injury. Our trainer always kept a bag in the infield during the game and another on his person when he was off the track. He would make a point of collecting wallets, rings, chains, earrings, and money clips from all the skaters and officials before the game. The track crew was warned as well about the no-jewelry rule, which included wedding bands. Nothing was sacred! So it was odd that on this particular morning, Dave failed to remove his wedding band. He simply forgot to do it.

I was working in the infield on the penalty boxes, when I saw Dave jump off the track from the high side with his hand on the top rail for balance. When he jumped down, his ring snagged on an upright bolt, and his finger was torn completely off, with only the bone remaining. I will never forget the sound of his screaming in agony as he jumped around while trying to tell me what had happened. As I ran toward the high end of the track, I saw his finger lying on the track near the infield. I picked it up, and at that moment, I realized what had happened. I started yelling for someone from the arena maintenance crew to call an ambulance. A couple of them ran down to the track, where I was comforting Dave, and told me that an ambulance was on the way. However, we didn't realize that there was a hospital just across the street.

Dave was going into shock, and I was not far behind. It was winter in Michigan, and the outside temperature was about 20 degrees Fahrenheit. The thought of taking Dave across the street to the emergency room in that freezing weather with his mangled hand seemed insane at first, but I remembered the power of ice on injuries, so I grabbed Dave along with one of the building people and took him across the street to the hospital. I asked another building person to call the hospital and tell them we were coming and that I had his finger with me. As soon as we stepped outside, I grabbed some snow and wrapped Dave's finger in my handkerchief. Then I tore off part of the sleeve from my sweatshirt, and with some snow, I wrapped up his hand.

Dave was hurting so bad that he kept telling me to knock him out. The thought had come to me as well, but he didn't need a broken jaw as well as a damaged hand. I know how hard it is to knock someone out so that he is rendered truly unconscious. That usually resulted in a concussion. So we escorted Dave to the hospital. The hospital personnel were not only waiting for us but also pushing a gurney down the emergency driveway toward us as we approached. The hospital staff took over while I supplied the details of the accident. At that moment, I realized that I still had Dave's finger wrapped in my handkerchief.

The nurse was happy to have the finger, and we were hopeful that the doctors could put it back on. I was shown to a waiting room, where I called Hal Janowitz, our road-trip manager, and told him what had happened and asked him to let J. J. Burton-Cannella know what was going on. In just a few minutes, the waiting room was full of skaters praying for Dave's speedy recovery.

I'm not sure how much time passed before a doctor came out to inform us that they had taken Dave's finger completely off to the last knuckle. Since the finger he'd lost was a ring finger, the removal would reduce his grip and make it difficult for him to shift gears in the truck. Remember—he not only was a referee but also earned his living driving our truck. The surgeon told us about a new, radical procedure that had helped other people with similar injuries. They could take off the little finger and use it to replace the ring finger. That would give his hand a stronger grip after a few months of physical therapy. We decided to wait a couple of days to tell Dave.

That night, it was hard to settle down and skate the game, even though we had a sold-out arena. The fans were going crazy. I had a hard time getting the day's images out of my head. While taking the track down that night, one of the crew was still wearing a wedding ring, and I went off on him. I told him to take it off, commenting that he didn't seem to understand what had just happened earlier in the day. A couple of teammates intervened to settle me down. I broke down and started crying like a baby. How could I have let something like that happen to my best friend? Even though others assured me it wasn't my fault, their reassurance didn't stop me from feeling responsible.

The team moved on to the next city while Dave remained in the hospital to have surgery on his hand. He was sent home for physical therapy and given time to recover. J. J. stayed with Dave for a couple of weeks and then rejoined us on the road. Dave was back driving the truck in a couple of months. He and I had a couple of beers at the first opportunity we had, and he assured me I hadn't done anything wrong. He insisted

I had done the right thing by wrapping his hand in snow and getting him to the hospital, not to mention trying to save his finger. Afterward, I felt better, but I will never forget that accident. I became a crusader for safety while skating or working on the track. I even lost two of my own wedding bands because I took them off, and they were subsequently stolen.

NUMBER 38, BILL GROLL, EX-MARINE

No one epitomizes a Roller Derby wannabe like Billy Groll. He ran away from life in Oakland, California, where he worked in construction as a laborer. After being discharged from the service, he spent every available night at the Roller Derby training center on 105th Avenue and East Fourteenth Street in Oakland. After closing, he would head to the bar to meet up with other Roller Derby skaters, including the greatest trackside announcer of our time, Donald Grey Drewry.

I met Bill while he was still in training school. I was on the Bay Bombers, while Bill had traveled down to Kezar Pavilion in San Francisco to skate in a minor-league game prior to the Bay Bombers versus New York Chiefs game taking place that evening. Bill was awkward and not totally balanced on his skates. However, he had heart and determination. He was the kind of guy you wanted to succeed, because he tried so hard.

Bill took some pretty bad falls and was run into the rails more than other minor-league skaters. But he kept getting up, and on sheer willpower, he would somehow find a way to score or at least block his opponent. The pros watching the game remarked, "Who is this kid?" Before long, Bill got a tryout with the New England Braves, and he never looked back.

Bill and I roomed together for part of a road trip in 1966. He spent a lot of time after the game with the night owls, but the late nights never seemed to slow him down. After tearing down the track, the crew would head to the hotel bar and party until closing, except when we had to immediately leave for the next city. Fortunately, Bill seldom brought anyone back to his room; instead, he elected to join the other guys and their girls in someone else's room.

After some investigation, I learned that all athletes are a little superstitious. The Roller Derby is no different. First of all, we never ate peanuts in the dressing room unless we wanted to break some body part that night. Secondly, we never talked about past injuries in the dressing room unless we wanted a trip home to heal up after breaking something. Thirdly, certain jersey numbers were bad luck. For the Bombers, it was number 38.

We were skating in Peoria, Illinois, and this was similar to our return trip after a couple of months on the road to Peoria again. I don't remember how it started, but Bill, wearing number 38, started talking about someone's past injury in this arena while he ate peanuts. Now, that was tempting fate. The call came into the dressing room for us to take the track for our warm-ups before the game. The warm-ups were going along normally, when Bill decided he wanted to take a whip from me so that he could go flying down the straightaway while doing a broadside sliding stop. I'm sure he did that to impress a couple of hot ladies sitting in the front row.

I started building up my speed with Bill right in back of me. As we came out of the turn, I reached back, and Bill took my hand. I did a 360-degree turn-and-stop, and Bill went flying around the outside, high on the track, doing at least forty miles per hour down the straightaway. Bill turned toward the infield part of the track while leaning and digging his wheels into the track like an ice-hockey-style stop. Unknown to either of us, there was a slick patch on the track where he was attempting to stop. Instead of stopping, his knee and ankle buckled, sending Bill home with a broken ankle as well as a broken leg. He didn't return until the regular season in the Bay Area, about four months later. He asked for a different jersey number when he returned.

Later that year, Bill met Beverly. She became Mrs. Groll, and we were all happy for him. Bev was just what Bill needed. She worked for Gillig Bus Company in Hayward, California. She was responsible and mature, and she loved Bill. He, in turn, decided to slow down the drinking and make a life with her. Bill went on to skate and coach, becoming one of our top skaters.

DRESSED TO KILL

We seldom had a night off. When we did, we wanted to dine in great restaurants, see a movie or a play, and have a few drinks. Afterward, Francine would go to a poker game, and I would drink, read, or watch TV. That was our normal routine. One night, we were in the beautiful city of Cleveland, Ohio—yes, I am being a bit sarcastic. In the late 1960s, Cleveland was not known for its beauty or its safety. I am glad to say that since then, the town has rebuilt itself and is now a beautiful city, not to mention a whole lot safer.

Francine and I ran into Nick Scopas and Joan Weston in the lobby of our hotel, so we decided to dine together. When we asked the front-desk clerk to recommend a five-star restaurant, he sent us to one right across the street from the hotel. Needless to say, we were skeptical, but he assured us it was safe, clean, and rated as one of the top places to dine in all of Cleveland. Since the area around the hotel was funky, we chose not to change into proper attire for five-star dining. Joanie was wearing blue jeans, a blouse covered by a sweater, and tennis shoes. Francine wore a nice skirt and blouse with dress shoes. We had just returned from a TV interview for the game. Nick was wearing blue jeans and a sweatshirt, while I was wearing dress pants and a nice blazer. As I said, we had been on display earlier and were dressed accordingly, but this was a restaurant that required men to wear ties.

You had to be there to appreciate the repartee when we entered the dining room. A pleasant maître 'd dressed in a fine suit with an outstanding tie greeted us. He took one look at us and didn't blink an eye while inquiring if we had reservations. We told him we did not and said that the hotel desk clerk had recommended his restaurant and that we wanted to dine where there was a great chef and a pleasant atmosphere. The maître 'd remarked to Nick and me that the dress code required men to wear proper ties. Without missing a beat, which was normal for Nick, he said I couldn't find one to match my sweatshirt. The maître 'd laughed and said he recognized us. We did notice that little twinkle that occurs when someone has recognized you.

He promptly seated us at a nice table, and the show began. Instantly, we had waiters bringing us water, bread, and butter, while another took our drink orders. Then, of course, the waiter made dinner suggestions. They had a great menu, and we couldn't believe the quality of the service and the atmosphere. After all, we were in a bad section of Cleveland, and here in this area was this little oasis of refinement and grace. Our dinners were incredible. Joanie and Francine had lobster with real Caesar salads made at our table from scratch. Nick and I had filet mignon and Caesar salads as well. For dessert, the girls had bananas flambé, while Nick and I had cherries jubilee. The experience was a pleasant surprise for all of us.

Before we finished, a few fans recognized Joanie, and she signed autographs, as did Nick, Francine, and I. The evening was a complete success. Before leaving, we arranged complimentary tickets for the maître 'd, the chef, and our waiters. Unfortunately, by the time we came back to Cleveland, that restaurant had closed. The front-desk clerk didn't know where the employees of that fine restaurant had gone. We had good memories that changed our attitude about skating in Cleveland.

DROP-KICKED IN CINCINNATI

Tonight we celebrate my daughter-in-law's birthday, and since I have a few minutes before the party, I will take some time to reflect on one of many concussions I received in the Roller Derby.

We were skating in Cincinnati, Ohio, against the Bay Bombers with Charlie O'Connell, Tony Roman, Gil Orozco, Joanie Weston, and others. My team, the Ohio Jolters, was leading in the derby standings. Our young team—including Margie Lazlo, Francine Cochu, Rosetta Saunders, Cliff Butler, Bobby Jennings, Jo Jo Stafford, and me, just to name a few—really wanted to win that pennant. The profession of skating had improved significantly. Everyone skated harder than before to ensure we would be victorious.

Normally, Charlie O. wouldn't stoop to dirty tactics to win. However, now, with only a few games left, Charlie's attitude was to win at any cost. I don't remember all the details, but we were just finishing up the first half, when I managed to score against Charlie. That was no easy task. Cliff dropped back to help, but Charlie took care of him in short order. As Cliff fell, I jumped over him while building up my speed. As I came out of the high part of the turn, I quickly squatted down and tucked into Charlie's inside, taking out his legs and causing him to take a hard fall. I called the jam off and was heading to the infield, when Charlie caught up with me. He grabbed me, spun me around, and hit me with a punch to my solar plexus, knocking the wind out of me. As I fell to the floor, he dropped-kicked me right on the chin.

I don't remember many of the details of the next four or five days. My teammates told me they helped me up after I came to. By then, I had caught my breath. They helped me off the track and into the dressing room. Andre Deek, our trainer, applied an ice pack to the back of my neck and rubbed my shoulders and neck. Then he had me lie down on the bench for a few minutes.

When the second half started, they left me in the dressing room to relax. However, by the time the men's period was starting, I was back on the track. I took a jammer's helmet and proceeded to alternate between jamming and blocking. My teammates told me they never saw me skate as hard and as viciously as I did that night. We won by six points. Between periods, the guys tried to talk with me, but I just shrugged them off while closing my eyes to rest with my head positioned against the back of the chair and a towel covering my face.

As we were leaving the track, I was climbing under the top rail and kickboard, when I passed out. The next thing I remember is waking up on a gurney in the hospital with Francine by my side. The next day, we traveled to a new city, but I don't recall where. I slept in the backseat the whole trip, and when I arrived in my hotel room, I went straight to bed. Francine had been instructed to make me stay awake as much as possible instead of letting me sleep all the time.

Hal Janowitz came by to pick up the cash and the leftover programs from the Cincinnati concession manager so that he could run my program concession while I recovered. Later, I took the reports and the cash to make a deposit at the bank, which, in turn, was wired to our Oakland headquarters. About a week after suffering the concussion, I got a call from our operations manager, asking about the receipts from the program sales. After going over my books with her, she commented about my concussion, remarking that she knew it must have been a bad one, because I had sent in over $1,500 too much. I then realized why my mad-money account was nearly empty.

During all my years in the Roller Derby, I know of four concussions I received, as well as numerous concussions of many other skaters. However, this one was the worst. I lost four or five days of my memory and was not 100 percent effective for a couple of months thereafter.

We won the pennant, but sadly, we lost the Roller Derby World Series when I failed to call off the last jam when I should have.

FARGO, NORTH DAKOTA

In 1965, as the reigning Rookie of the Year, I was really full of myself. After all, I had skated for the Chicago Pioneers with Coach Bert Wall and had won the coveted award after besting several good skaters. The truth was that I was versatile, a good skater, a journeyman carpenter, and a backyard mechanic, in addition to having a couple of years in college under my belt. Oh, and I had moved every few months for my entire life, so road trips were easy for me. I could skate, work on the track crew, and manage the sale and administration of Roller Derby programs, and I was a good driver who didn't require much sleep. I was perfect. Where else could you get all of those skills for merely sixty-five dollars a week for skating and $125 a week for working on the track crew and acting as program manager? Throw TV, radio, and newspaper interviews into the mix, and I was a bargain.

Now, on with the Fargo story. I was smart enough to know that I needed to learn more and perform better than my competitors. After driving straight through from Reno, Nevada, after skating a game and tearing down the track, I had about five hours of sleep in Fargo before going to the auditorium to set up the track and work on my jumping ability. In Reno, after I missed a jump over a fallen skater, Charlie O'Connell yelled at me to learn how to jump over, skate around, or miss a fallen skater. My plan was to practice jumping over the folding chairs used in the infield of the track. First, I set up one chair on its side (about eighteen inches high) and made several easy jumps at speed over the obstacle. Next, I stood the chair up with its back toward me, and while skating at speed, I was able to jump the chair cleanly. Then

I set up two chairs back-to-back and did the jumping drill again. Then I tried three chairs, with just a little clip of my skates against the first chair. I followed with four chairs, again with only a little nick of my skates against the first chair. Finally, when I attempted to jump five chairs, I wiped out. My skate caught the first chair and sent me crashing into the fifth chair. This sent me flying into the rail. For this effort, I split my lip and banged up my knee and shin while demolishing a chair.

I picked myself up and went to the bathroom to wash the blood off my legs and rinse out my mouth and my pride. When I returned to the track, the broken chair was still lying on the track, along with the other four chairs. A janitor from the building was standing nearby. Apparently, he had been watching and had come down from the balcony to see how I was. I apologized for damaging the chair and offered to pay for it. He said not to worry, because he could replace it from the storeroom. He was certain nothing would happen.

Well, that night, after warming up for the game, we came back into the dressing room, and Charlie asked if anyone had been down at the building during the afternoon jumping chairs. Of course I spoke up and recounted what had happened. He was angry because the building manager was upset that I had been skating on the track without supervision, which was a legal liability for the City of Fargo since they owned the building. Additionally, there was the matter of the broken metal chair and who was going to pay for it. I spoke up and apologized, offering to pay for the chair, which, at fifty dollars, was almost a week's pay for skating. Hal Janowitz, our box-office manager, said he would write a check to the city, and the matter was resolved. On my next paycheck, there was a fifty-dollar deduction, and someone had drawn a little chair on my check. I suspect Hal was the artist. I learned that being the Rookie of the Year didn't mean a thing when it came to keeping building managers and cities happy. Later, in 1967, when I ran the training school in Montreal, I used highway safety cones for jumping purposes. If someone was caught stealing the traffic cones, there was a $500 fine. Some things are just worth the risk.

By the way, I never kicked another skater in the head while jumping a fallen skater. As a matter of fact, I was well known for my jumping ability.

FOUR-STORY DIVING BOARD, OR HOW TO JUMP OFF THE ROOF OF THE HOLIDAY INN AND LIVE

In 1964, 1965, and 1966, we stayed at the same Holiday Inn in Omaha, Nebraska. It featured a pool in the center of the U-shaped building, perfect for jumping off the handrails into the swimming pool—or, if you were really drunk, jumping off the roof into the pool. That's right! That's what bored Roller Derby skaters did with their time off. We would have a few too many beers and then go swimming. Of course, if you swim, you have to go diving into the pool.

I think the Hawaiian kids started the diving ritual first, but we haoles didn't wait long to take up the challenge. Soon we were diving into the pool from the higher floors. We were lucky that the hotel was only four stories high. It took three years before management banned us from this hotel. We were fortunate that no one was seriously injured. You sometimes hear of people breaking their necks in backyard pools when simply diving from a diving board, and here we were, diving from forty-plus feet into an eight-feet-deep pool. God was clearly watching over us.

GEORGE "RUN-RUN" JONES

During my rookie year, I had the pleasure—and sometimes pain—of rooming with George Jones, or, as most people knew him, Run-Run or just Runner. I say it was sometimes a pain because he was a big pain in the backside when he was drunk, which was most of the time. When he was sober, he was still a pain but not as bad. George had been a Roller Derby star in the 1950s and early '60s but had gotten into some kind of trouble and was now, in 1964, getting a chance to skate again.

George had the endurance of an elk, with the ability to skate for hours at a steady pace. One of the training drills we did to build endurance and speed was to skate in a line around the track like a train. The person in front set the pace, and everyone had to keep up, or the person behind would run him or her over or be forced to fall back. So every person was responsible for keeping up with the person in front and staying ahead of the person behind. George could set a blistering pace of twenty-five to thirty miles per hour and keep that pace up for twenty to thirty minutes. Normally, a pace would be for a fifteen-minute interval with a five-lap sprint at the end and then a twenty-minute break, followed by another drill.

Usually, the person in front would drop off by heading high into the turn and letting the others pass by before rejoining the group at the end of the pace line. George would never relinquish the front position, and his pace was so fast that many would have to drop out to catch their breath before joining the line again. As a rookie, I had to stay with him till the bitter end. Fortunately, I had been a cross-country runner and had run the mile on my high-school track team.

George was in great shape for a guy who was in his thirties, drank every night, and usually brought women back to the room to screw till dawn. I believe George was born in Moline, Illinois, and he had a brother and other family members who often attended the games in Moline and Chicago. Bert Wall would let George jam in those towns, and he always scored well on the track as well as off. George skated until 1967 before retiring to the San Francisco Bay Area. He landed a job as an equipment helper for a new football team—the Oakland Raiders.

George worked for the Raiders until his death in 2007. We all got a kick out of watching George run out to the players with water bottles during the time-outs. He always knew where to stand on the sidelines to get the most camera time. Twice, he got me into a game using a press pass. I got to enjoy the game while sitting in the press booth at the Oakland Coliseum. After the game, I was invited into the dressing room. What a treat that was! I met Kenny Stabler, George Blanda, and Fred Biletnikoff. Knowing George had perks.

One time, after a four-week stint in the Pacific Northwest, we were traveling to Corpus Christi, Texas, and we had barely enough time to drive there before our scheduled game. Some of the stars were sent ahead via the airlines, but George; Terry Smith; Don Drewry, our announcer; and I had to drive the George-mobile, a rusty old van with a bed in the back instead of seats. We were told not to stop off in the Bay Area, even though we would have to pass through the region. Needless to say, we stopped off in Oakland while George went to his girlfriend's house for a home-cooked meal and God knows what else. Don Drewry stopped by to see his mom and have a meal with her while Terry and I went to Mr. and Mrs. Keenon's home for a meal with the family that had kindly taken me in when I was living in my car.

Larry Smith

George was two hours late picking us up, and we were already four hours behind schedule. George had had a couple of drinks but insisted on driving. He refused to take Highway 99, the most direct route to Los Angeles, where we could connect with Highway 10 to Texas. George decided to take Highway 35, which is a two-lane road winding through San Joaquin County and all the small towns. Finally, when we got close to Bakersfield, George got sleepy, and I was able to drive.

We arrived in Corpus Christi at about five o'clock in the evening, just in time to help set up the track. This was fortunate because we needed the extra pay. By the time we finished, we only had enough time for a couple of trackside steaks, otherwise known as hot dogs, for our only meal of the day. I don't remember much of that game, only that I kept falling and tripping over my feet. George claimed he had a stomachache right after warm-ups and went to sleep in his car. That left us shorthanded on jammers, and since I was the hot-dog rookie, I got to skate every jam. I don't remember the teardown of the track after the game or the bar or motel time afterward. I was in a fog for two or three days. George, on the other hand, was back to his old self the next day. That's George "Run-Run" Jones.

GETTING MARRIED IN RENO

Francine Cochu was a star from the beginning of her Roller Derby career, even in training school. She and Judy Sinnet were moved to the men's training squad because of their speed and ability to block and maneuver. From the first time I saw her, I was overwhelmed with romantic feelings. Many times, in my quest to capture the true Roller Derby spirit, I proclaimed my love for Francine, so it was no surprise that we decided to marry.

The surprise was in the timing. Our wedding was thrust upon us after a game in Omaha, Nebraska. We were told that operations would be suspended until mid-January. We traveled to Chicago for a game; had a match in Pittsburgh, Pennsylvania; and then drove all the way back to the San Francisco Bay Area. Francine and Judy were sent back to their homes in Canada, while I continued on to Los Angeles for a six-game series against the Los Angeles Thunderbirds of the Roller Games League. There was a chance that Francine and Judy would not return for the January tour. This absence would stop them from skating full-time, which worried them. In a crowded little hotel bar in Chicago, I asked Francine for a dance to Tony Bennett's rendition of "I Left My Heart in San Francisco." I proposed to her on that dance floor, and she said yes.

The bar was full of skaters, and the news was electrifying. Everyone, though saddened by the suspension, started singing and slapping us on the back. They bought us drinks while asking about our wedding plans. Needless to say, I didn't have a clue. By the time we closed the bar, we had the plans all worked out. Francine, Bill Morrissey, John Early, Frank

Mello, and I would drive in my car to the San Francisco Bay Area by the northern Reno route. There Francine and I could get our marriage license and get married. Afterward, I would drop Francine off in San Leandro, California, and continue on to Los Angeles for the Roller Games series. All was well.

The trip was fairly uneventful, except for the snowstorms. I skated in the Chicago game and then worked the track crew before grabbing three hours of sleep. I drove to Pittsburgh to set up the track, skated, and then tore down the track before getting behind the wheel to start the 2,400-mile trip to Reno. On the way, I got some relief from driving and got another three hours of sleep. When we arrived in Reno at four o'clock in the afternoon, I had been up for more than seventy hours. I was working on adrenaline.

We checked into a hotel in Reno, with plans to arrive at the courthouse just in time to get a marriage license before booking a wedding chapel. Our plan was to get married and have dinner with the group, and then Francine and I would sleep—after all, it was our honeymoon. The next morning, we would continue our trip to San Leandro. Francine and I went to our room to dress before going to the courthouse while Bill Morrissey made arrangements with a wedding chapel. The other guys started the champagne party early.

Francine started crying as soon as we got into the room, and I couldn't understand why. I thought she might be getting cold feet. I finally understood what she was so upset about: she had forged the date on her birth certificate in order to qualify for the Roller Derby training school and acquire a professional skating position. She was only seventeen at the present time. The State of Nevada required a person to be at least eighteen years old to marry. I thought we should go to the courthouse and attempt to get married using the forged birth certificate. We did, and the state issued our marriage license without a problem.

When we returned from the courthouse, we went up to our room so that Francine could change for the wedding. She started crying again. I thought, *Here we go again. She must be getting cold feet.* It seems that in her rush to get her luggage transferred from Joan Weston's car to my car while we were in Pittsburgh, she had not grabbed the bag with the dress and shoes she wanted to wear. She only had sneakers. It was six o'clock, and most of the shoe stores I called were already closed. Finally, I found a store where, even though it was closed, someone answered the phone. He agreed to let me come down to buy Francine a new pair of shoes.

We had reserved a typical Reno wedding chapel for a 6:30 p.m. ceremony. We didn't want to be late, so we drove like crazy to get there on time. We barely made it. The minister was ready, and Bill Morrissey was my best man. John Early and Frank Mello were flower girls for Francine. Everyone got a chuckle out of that one. During the ceremony, Francine kept saying, "I will," every time the minister paused. After all, French was her native language, and she was not completely in command of English. The photographer we hired was a little drunk and kept telling me to grab Francine's butt as she took photos, which we never received. I wonder how they turned out.

After the ceremony, we all went back to the hotel and had champagne with our dinner. I was starting to fall asleep, and poor Francine was tired as well. The guys accused us of just wanting to start our honeymoon. The truth was, we were so tired that we went to the room, gave each other a kiss, and went right to sleep. The next morning, we got up early and drove to San Leandro. I rented a kitchenette at the Nimitz Motel after we got there. It was only a couple of hours until I met up with a few other skaters, and we drove to Los Angeles.

I made Frank Mello and John Early promise to take Francine out for a nice dinner a couple of times while I was in Los Angeles. She reported that they were perfect gentlemen. The joining of our spirits might not have been the most romantic, but we were married for seventeen years and raised two wonderful children: Charles Anthony, who is now thirty-six years old and has a wonderful wife named Christy and an eight-month-old daughter named Zoey, and my daughter, Jacqueline Kay, is now thirty-one years old and a college graduate.

For the record, Francine and I have remained the best of friends, and her current husband, Steve, and I are good friends as well. Our kids cannot understand how we kept our friendship alive with love for one another throughout the divorce.

I LOST MY SMILE IN JACKSONVILLE

It was 1968, and we were skating in Atlanta, Georgia. I was on the Bay Bombers, and we were playing against the New York Chiefs. Ronnie Robinson and Margie Lazlo were the stars of their team. Our men's coach was Charlie O'Connell, and Joan Weston was the women's captain. During the last few weeks of our tour with the Chiefs, I had trouble with Allen Little of the Chiefs. We would end up in a fight every night. One night, he would kick the crap out of me. The next night, I would do the same to him.

There wasn't anything special about this game. The lead was going back and forth, when I scored three points by passing Ronnie, Allen, and Pete Boyd. The memorable part was that Charlie had set Pete up for me. I squatted low and took out his legs as I went by. Then Charlie knocked the crap out of Allen as Ronnie came back to help him. When Charlie moved out of the way, Ronnie hit Allen, and I jumped over them as they fell. I called off the jam, stopping in the turn up high while talking to a fan. The next thing I knew, Ronnie came up behind me and pinned my arms to my side. Before I could respond, Allen came in and punched me square in the mouth. I dropped like a brick. Then they both kicked me several times. The next thing I remember is the trainer holding smelling salts under my bloody nose. Boy, my mouth was throbbing.

After a few minutes with an ice pack on my mouth and nose, I skated the last period of the game and scored more points. We ended up losing that game to the Chiefs. I didn't work on the track crew that night, but

I did check in with the concession manager regarding the programs and then went to a restaurant with Francine and a few other skaters. I tried to eat, but my mouth was swollen and hurt like hell. That night, we left for Jacksonville, Florida, for a matinee game. By the time I got to the hotel in Jacksonville, my front teeth had started abscessing, so I asked the hotel manager about a dentist. It was Sunday morning, and we had a game at two o'clock that afternoon, so time was of the essence.

The hotel manager called a golfing buddy who was a dentist, and he agreed to meet me at his office, which was only a few miles away. The dentist examined my two front teeth and gums and determined it would take an operation to save my loose teeth, and he had to drain the abscess right away before the infection got any worse. The other option was to pull my front teeth now and give me some medication so that I would be able to rest. I was not scheduled for a game that day, and since I didn't want to go home for the operation and leave Francine on the road alone, I told him to pull the teeth. He drained my abscessed gums, which is something I hope never to have done again. Then he explained that it was better to pull the teeth without giving me any more medication beforehand, since the shots would hurt more than the actual pulling of the teeth. Looking back, I wish I had elected for the shots.

Just like in a movie comedy, he climbed up onto my lap in order to hold me down and then proceeded to pull the teeth out—both at the same time. It's a good thing he was a large man, because it took all his strength and my willpower to stay in the chair while he pulled those teeth out. I bled like a stuffed pig, so he had to sew up my gums to stop the bleeding. By now, my swollen mouth, broken nose, and darkening eyes from the broken nose made me look like a prizefighter who had lost the fight after going fifteen rounds. Needless to say, I was glad I didn't have to skate that night. At least I thought I didn't have to skate.

The doctor gave me medication to ease the swelling and prevent infection and another pill for the pain. When I got back to our room, Francine was frightened when she saw me. I couldn't explain well, so I took more pills and went straight to bed with a rag full of ice to reduce the swelling. Later, she woke me up to say that the team needed me to skate because two of our male skaters had come down with a bad virus. They were throwing up and couldn't keep anything down. That meant we only had four men left who were able to skate.

So I took more pain pills. When I looked in the mirror, I saw that I looked like a raccoon. I knew what I needed to do, so I got my gear and then went to the arena with Francine. When we arrived, we went straight to our respective dressing rooms. I put an ice pack on my face and then dressed early before lying down on a bench. I guess I must have looked pretty bad, because a steady line of skaters came by for a look. We decided to put some makeup on my black eyes so that I wouldn't scare the children.

I don't remember much about that game; I don't even know if we won. With only five skaters, I had to alternate between blocking and jamming. I was knocking the crap out of everyone, even my own teammates. The pain pills were doing their job, and I was flying high.

Three weeks later, I had an impression made for new teeth in Macon, Georgia. Since we were scheduled to return the next week for another game, I would have the new teeth when I returned to Georgia. In the meantime, I lived without front teeth. I learned not to smile during TV interviews. I also learned not to talk much, since I was having trouble enunciating words properly. When we got back to Macon, the dentist had my new teeth ready, and they fit pretty well. As a matter of fact, I kept those teeth for eight more years, until I lost more teeth when I didn't duck a punch in time.

Someday I hope to have a new set of teeth made to fill in all the holes left from my days in the Roller Derby. Then I will be able to smile again.

JERRY

The Monday afternoon after Thanksgiving, the office was abuzz with everyone trying to make last-minute sales. I was working on my buyers and sellers to make things happen now. Our market continued to be soft, and the prospect of it changing for the better anytime soon was slim. Diane Sass and I spent our holiday with my aunt Ruth and her children in Clovis, California. On Friday, we went to my uncle Merle's home in Exeter, California, for what could have been my last visit. He was losing his battle with cancer, and his wife, Murrieta, was struggling with the maladies of old age. Making the trip even more challenging, my sister went to the hospital with pneumonia on Thursday night. Our trip was one filled with compassion and thanks for those who helped us throughout the years.

This morning, Diane handed me a copy of the *Contra Costa Valley Times* newspaper, which featured an article about the new Roller Derby, naming James Fitzpatrick as the general manager of the new Bay Bombers and the new Roller Derby league. I was glad they were keeping Leo's dream alive.

It is time for one of the more difficult stories to tell. Jerry Cartell was an Oakland policeman when I met him. He was skating on several teams in the Bay Area when they came into town. It was common for a team owner to hire local talent to skate in the Bay Area rather than fly in someone from the East Coast. Jerry gave off a spoiled-bad-boy image with talent. The women loved him because he was six foot two, weighed in at two hundred pounds, and had blond hair and a great smile. Under that smile was the heart of a gay man. Jerry was fired from the police force and subsequently joined the sheriff's department of Alameda County, California. One could only guess the reason. Remember this was the late 1960s, and being gay was not an in thing to be, especially on the police force.

Jerry and I skated on the Ohio Jolters together in 1972. He was a good teammate, and I never had a problem with him. However, when I skated against him, it was a different story. He was a tough skater to pass and would use his right skate to kick people in the groin or the shins to stop them from scoring. I've had my share of fights with Jerry, and once, in Fresno, California, in front of my family, Jerry was kicking the crap out of me, when I lost control and started punching him back. We ended up in the infield, going toe-to-toe. Jerry not only had the height advantage but also was wearing a football helmet with a face guard because of a prior broken nose. I finally kicked him where he had been kicking me. When his knees buckled, he was at my height, so I hit him in the throat and the solar plexus. He stopped throwing punches. The referees subsequently broke up the fight.

The next major fight was a few months later in Atlanta. We were skating on opposite teams, when Jerry, for no apparent reason, tried to catch me at the infield table while I was getting attention for an injury. He came right off the top of the high side of the track and went full speed through the infield, headed straight for me. Our trainer yelled at me just in time so that I could set myself up for the attack. I caught Jerry with one hand on his throat and the other on his groin, and then I did a judo throw, tossing Jerry into the empty ladies' bench. He landed in the chairs and then careened into the penalty box, tumbling a couple of times before coming to a stop. The referees grabbed me before I could inflict any more damage. Jerry ended up with a bad cut over one eye that required stitches. I really had no reason to hurt him, but I did get pleasure from reversing the outcome he had planned for me.

I haven't seen or heard from Jerry since 1973. Just the other day, I received an e-mail from Bill Accord, asking me if he could give Jerry my e-mail address. I thought long and hard before saying yes. Now I'm watching out for him to sneak up on me for payback.

Several skaters met at Harry's Hofbrau in San Leandro for a retirement dinner in honor of Delores "Tilly" Tucker, a former Bay Bomber from the late 1960s and early 1970s. Tilly was a good skater. She was quiet and professional and never displayed the need to be the star. She had great team spirit. I admired her for that. Talking with her, I realized she had been on the janitorial service at the Kaiser Hospital for twenty-five years. Now she was retiring from that position and just wanted to relax, work in her yard, and enjoy life.

To my surprise, Jerry was there with a younger friend, and he seemed truly happy to see me. I was happy too. Despite my reluctance, we shared a few stories about the good old days and what we were doing now. He owns a store that sells bicycles, sporting goods, and adventure-trip supplies. He said the business was doing okay, and he was happy with his life. I was happy for him too.

On February 17, 2013, some skaters from the Roller Derby and Roller Games met at Harry's Hofbrau in San Leandro for a reunion. This seems to be evolving into a recurring event every three or four months. I was late getting there, but Jerry and Bill Accord saved me a seat. We talked about the Roller Derby days and reminisced with the Roller Games skaters about the good old days. We enjoyed another quarterly reunion with some of the skaters from my time with the Roller Derby. We started having meetings at Harry's Hofbrau in San Leandro every few months. We tell the new skaters from the Roller Games League stories about how it was. They enjoy hearing them as much as we enjoy telling them. Of course, we are all better skaters in our minds than we actually were on the field of play. Back in our time, the fights were bigger, and the games were harder.

JOHN "PORKY" PARKER— UTICA, NEW YORK

In 1965 in Utica, New York, John "Porky" Parker, Eddie Krebs, and I had a run-in at the arena downtown. Eddie and I had finished setting up the track and decided to hang around to practice some new moves. Eddie was five or six years older than I was and had a lot more skating experience. I wanted to be the best, so I routinely asked more-experienced skaters to show me some new moves. Eddie had a big ego and was always ready to tell anyone how good he was. We had become friends, so he taught me how to get more speed and how to set a guy up with a right elbow and then a quick left elbow to his ribs. This maneuver made other skaters think twice before trying to pass on the inside. It also made it easier to knock someone down if he tried to get by me on the outside. About the same time, I learned that a hip check at the right moment, followed by a quick right and then left elbow, would send other skaters over the rail. This tactic allowed me the opportunity to score without having to worry about the other jammer.

After working out, Eddie and I went into the dressing room to shower and change clothes. While we were in there, we could hear Porky in the other dressing room, singing. Apparently, as we learned later, he had come to the arena to do a newspaper and TV interview. Now, keep in mind that Porky had no clue we were in the other room, because we kept quiet as soon as we heard someone singing. The heating ductwork was easily accessible. Eddie, being the smart one of the group, learned how to use Aqua Net hair spray and a cigarette lighter as a torch. All you had to do was start spraying the alcohol-based hair spray, light the lighter, and hold it at the edge of the spray, and like magic, you had created a torch.

This was shaping up to be a memorable day; I'd learned the right-left elbow combination with a hip check that guaranteed a knockdown of any opponent, and in addition, I had an automatic torch at my disposal since I always used Aqua Net hair spray, which acted like a chemical helmet if you used enough of that stuff on your hair. Now I could use it in dressing-room fights as well. Yeah!

Now back to Porky. Eddie convinced me to shoot a flame from our torch into the ductwork vent. Of course, that would cause flames to shoot out the other side of the vent into Porky's side of the dressing room. I had heard that Porky liked a good joke as well as the next person, so with Eddie cheering me on, I stood on a chair, pushed on the spray nozzle, and lit the flame. Wow, what a flame!

Instantly, we heard Porky scream, curse, and then get up and head straight for our side of the dressing room. The next thing I knew, Porky charged in, yelling at the top of his lungs. He had big lungs. As a matter of fact, John was a big man. He stood six foot two and weighed in at 275 pounds, which was big for a skater. When he burst in, I fell off the chair, almost setting him on fire since I was still holding the flaming torch.

When Eddie saw all of this, he fell down on the floor laughing. Imagine this picture: Porky Parker was wearing a new suit and tie while covered from head to toe in black soot from the ductwork. His white shirt was nearly black, the tie was completely ruined, and the suit coat was coated in black ash. To make matters worse, he hadn't completed the interviews. That meant he would have to reschedule or cancel the TV interview. About this time, the newspaper columnist arrived to do the newspaper interview. He started laughing when he realized what had happened. Eddie got control of his laughter and recounted the story to the reporter, who ate it up. Before Porky could stop him, the reporter took a couple of photos and began busily writing notes for his article.

Next, the TV crew arrived to shoot the TV interview. When they saw Porky and heard Eddie's version of the story, they started laughing as well. Porky was mad. He didn't have a change of clothes, so Eddie and I offered to do the interview. When the reporters accepted our offer, Porky became even madder.

Eddie and I did the interview, while Porky went straight to a telephone. In a few minutes, Hal Janowitz, our road-trip manager, arrived in the building to hear Porky's side of the story. Afterward, he heard Eddie's version and started laughing, which made Porky more upset. Porky's suit was ruined, and he didn't get to do the interview. Needless to say, Eddie and I turned over most of our pay the following week as restitution. Keep in mind that Porky loved to gamble and bet on the ponies. He probably lost the money we gave to him on some old nag, because Porky never bought a new suit as far as we knew.

I should point out here that the laughter caused by our prank and the fun it created when the story was retold became a team tradition. In the end, everyone knew how to make a hair-spray torch. The hair-spray torch was a hot item for a long time. Eventually, Mr. Parker forgave me, and we had a good laugh over a couple of beers at the racetrack.

"LARAPIN" LOU DONOVAN

There has never been a man, skater, or entertainer like Lou Donovan. He lived to gross everyone out with the things he said, the things he ate, or the tricks he would try just to get a reaction. He got the nickname Kamikaze because he would purposely take rails by running into or crashing over or through them. He would dive into the center trainer's table, try to jump infield chairs, jump into the crowd, or pick his bloody scabs just to make them bleed.

One time, we were opening a new arena, and the mayor's wife was invited to sound the starting whistle. As gross as it is, this is a true story. During the warm-up period, the referees would stay in the dressing room to prepare for the upcoming game. Lou, upon hearing about the mayor's wife, wiped his butt with the whistle that she would use. Yuck! We tried to talk him out of this, and Bill Morrissey, the other referee, said he would give his whistle to the mayor's wife. However, Lou beat him to it. Thank God only a few of us were aware of what was going on. Mrs. Mayor listened to the announcer as he told everyone about the honor being bestowed on her and invited her to blow the whistle as loudly as she could to start the game. She did. She wrapped her lips around that whistle as if it were a hot dog, took a deep breath, and then let it out. The girls started skating and almost ran over her because she was standing on the edge of the track. Lou walked over to her, took the whistle from her hand, and threw it into the trash can. He then took a fresh whistle from his pocket. At that moment, I think she must have realized what had just happened. She never said a word and waited for the girls' pack to pass her on the turn. She then walked across the track, ducked under the rail, and exited the building without looking back.

Once, in Cincinnati, the Ohio Jolters were playing two games against the Bay Bombers over a weekend. Lou loved bratwurst hot dogs with sauerkraut and onions. He said they made the most gas—and he was right. The upside meant washing each brat down with as many beers as possible. On Friday night, before the game, during the game, and after the game, Lou ate at least eight brats. All of them were loaded with sauerkraut, onions, and chili. That's right! He convinced the concessionaire to include chili on the brats.

After the game, Lou went out to a beer joint and got stinking drunk—no pun intended. By game time on Saturday, Lou was ripe. During the first men's-period jam, Lou broke out behind me with a strong whip from Gil Orozco and then passed me on the outside in the straightaway—something that you just don't do. I gave him a hip check, which sent him flying over the rail, and he landed hard on the concrete floor, causing him to pass a massive amount of gas. The people in the first couple of rows where Lou landed were coughing and gagging. The skaters who knew what was happening were laughing so hard that they had a hard time staying in their chairs. A couple of jams later, Lou broke out on a jam with me in hard pursuit. Lou cut loose, and I swear there was a green fog behind Lou. As I skated through it, I almost gagged. By the time the pack caught up to the foggy mist, they were all coughing and gagging.

Lou had done it. The entire pack was suffering from his gaseous attacks. The poor fans had no clue why we were all laughing so hard. At one point, Lou broke out on a jam, and guess who was on his tail. Charlie stopped the whole pack, performing a subway, where everyone piles on each other. Then the pack stopped in its tracks, allowing Lou to catch up with the pack sooner. When the Jolters realized this, they all got up and did a pull-away. The whole pack skated away at top speed from Lou.

By halftime, Lou was asked to stay in the dressing room while one of the rookies skated in his place. Lou was the king.

Another Donovan tale occurred in Richmond, California, at the auditorium. Earlier in the day, Lou, Gil Orozco, Bill Morrissey, and I were working on the track, conducting major repairs, checking for cracked rails and worn spots in the track, and doing a general safety check. Lou and I were checking the top rails and found one that needed to be replaced before the game that night. Lou convinced me to keep quiet about the rail, because he wanted to take that rail out during the game. This was something that was not allowed because of the danger to skaters. But I agreed to remain quiet about this risk. Lou made a slight mark on the upright holding the rail so that he would know which part of the rail to hit.

I held my breath during the first women's period, fearing someone would hit that rail and get hurt. However, providence was on our side. As we started the men's period, Lou asked me to point out the proper rail. Lou needed glasses but was too vain to wear them. I showed him the marked rail, and as we skated off to join the pack, I wondered how he would be able to hit that rail at exactly the right spot to take it out.

Well, after a couple of jams with Lou trying to put himself into position to take out the rail, nothing had happened. I was concerned that someone else might end up taking out the rail and getting hurt. In Lou's case, he planned on hitting it straight-on, taking the rail completely off, and landing in the crowd.

Near the end of the first period, Lou got his chance. The pack was coming out of the turn just as the starting whistle blew, and Gil Orozco led Lou out of the pack. Gil was going to give Lou a whip, and no one was more powerful at giving a whip than Gil. As they broke from the pack, Lou was stretching as far as he could to maximize the power of the whip. Gil, with his hand in Lou's, reached back with all his force and did a turn-and-throw, pulling on Lou's hand as he released. Lou flew down the straightaway right into a rail with both arms cupped under the rail, and his chest slammed into the two-by-four. Lou was expecting the rail to give way, so he hit it as hard as he could with his rib cage exposed.

The rail didn't budge, and the force stopped Lou. We could hear a couple of ribs crack. Lou slid down to the track surface with a pained expression on his face, trying to catch his breath. Charlie O'Connell skated up to Lou and jumped up on the rail. As he started to ask Lou if he was okay, the rail gave way, and Charlie fell onto the track. By this time, I was on the track, talking to Lou while the trainer was getting the stretcher for him. Lou was headed to the hospital. As Lou was taken away on the stretcher, he looked at me with a "What happened?" expression on his face. I mouthed to him, "Wrong rail!" A few days later, we had a couple of beers and a good laugh over that. Lou finally broke down and got glasses when he started to referee.

KU KLUX KLAN AND THE 1960S

For many reasons, I have put off writing about this time in America and how it impacted those of us in the Roller Derby. It is difficult to filter my feelings from fact and the media's interpretation of facts and the feelings of those who lived through this period in America. In the '60s, race was an issue. In the Deep South, we played cities with billboards proclaiming, "You are now in Ku Klux Klan Country," and we saw separate Laundromats for blacks and whites. We also encountered separate drinking fountains and building entrances, hotels that segregated our skaters, and bars that refused to serve them. We skated at arenas and auditoriums with segregated dressing rooms, and blacks and whites riding in the same car together was unthinkable—it was just not done.

My father raised me to believe that all people were equal. However, you didn't cross the lines. Girls and boys didn't date across ethnic lines. Dad would boast about how he had shared a cigarette with black GIs when he was in the army. After all, his buddy was protecting his backside and his life. After the service, Dad worked at a munitions plant in Martinez, California, and there was a no-smoking policy, as you certainly can understand. However, the men would take smoke breaks outside of the storage buildings, and Dad would usually end up sharing a smoke with his black coworker. He'd always say, "It didn't bother him."

When I was growing up, we were beyond poor. We were living in government housing, moving three or four times a year, and doing migrant working jobs until I was about twelve years old. Then Dad went into the carpentry business with his two brothers. During those poor days, at eight years old, I picked cotton with my stepsister and stepbrother during Christmas vacation in Farmersville, California. Dad had sewn two potato sacks together to make a cotton-picking sack for me. I was too young to live by myself while the family worked, and besides, the $1.00 to $1.50 I made went into our cookie jar for necessities. I was proud that I could contribute. It taught me that no matter my color, I was able and required to earn my keep.

During the early years in my training-school days at 105th Avenue and East Fourteenth Street in Oakland, Cliff Butler and I became best friends. Later, we skated together on the Bay Bombers and the Ohio Jolters. Cliff was black, and he and I loved to scuba dive together in Monterey, California. While we were getting certified as scuba divers at the Anchor Shack in Hayward, owned by Bob Hollis of Scuba Pro Company fame, we were required to practice mouth-to-mouth resuscitation, and since we were dive partners and friends, it didn't enter into our thoughts that Cliff was the only black diver.

The training program required us to monitor each other's well-being in the water, so when it came time to practice the mouth-to-mouth technique needed to save your partner's life, Cliff and I had no reservations: we were two guys doing what would have to be done in an emergency. We were not gay, but it was a bit awkward. Later, we talked about it as we drove to Monterey for a day of spearfishing; it was the first real talk we had about race.

I think our friendship was enhanced by the race issue—not only on the track but also through our diving days. We always got a laugh at the looks other divers gave Cliff and me when we would suit up. Back then, you didn't see black divers on the beach. It was weird. I was living in San Leandro, and Cliff lived in Berkeley. The issues about race were going on all around us. We had made up several jokes and punch lines about the situation. I would remind Cliff to smile when we were in the water and the visibility was poor so that I could see him. He would tell me that when he was a shark, he was going to shoot me with his spear gun and swim to shore. Since sharks prefer white meat, he would be able to get safely to shore.

Some of the divers we hooked up with were from the South. They quickly realized how special Cliff was. Not only did he have a great diving ability, but also, his wonderful sense of humor put him off the charts. Sometimes if they continued staring, he would challenge them with "Haven't you seen a black diver before?" Then he would give that big smile of his, and all was well.

In the hotels, we had to change sleeping arrangements since some of the black girls roomed with white girls, and the same was true for the men. This was not allowed in the South, where hotels were segregated. When we dined at Holiday Inns, they normally allowed the white and black skaters to sit at the same table—usually. In a couple of locations, such as Fayetteville, South Carolina, black skaters had to eat in their rooms because the hotel operator was afraid some of his friends would find out that he rented rooms to blacks in an all-white hotel.

Dressing rooms were always an issue. Most venues had two large dressing rooms: one for the home team and one for the visitors. Since both men and women skated in the Roller Derby, the dressing rooms were split by sex: one for the men and one for the women. There were no additional rooms to segregate blacks from whites. You might have noticed I haven't mentioned anything about the Mexican skaters. Sometimes they were treated as if they were black, while other times it was okay for them to be with whites. It's a good thing they didn't know about gay skaters in the Roller Derby. My God, what a mess that could have been.

I especially remember Charlie O'Connell giving Ronnie Robinson, a black skater and the son of the original great fighter, Sugar Ray Robinson, a bad time in Mobile, Alabama. In that game, Charlie was knocking the crap out of Ronnie. Normally, it was the other way around. Charlie would eventually win the battle by outskating Ronnie, winning points and throwing in a good punch or two to win the fight. When we were in the South, Ronnie could not be allowed to succeed. Charlie knocked the stuffing out of him, and Ronnie was too afraid to really fight back. The southern fans loved it, of course. Don't feel sorry for Ronnie, because when we went back up north, he got even with Charlie.

It was sad how racism was dividing our country. As athletes, we respected the other person's ability and heart. We didn't care what color people's skin was or what religion they practiced. We did have some problems with the gay thing if they started flaunting it, but for the most part, we all got along. Later, toward the end of the Roller Derby era that I knew, between the 1950s and 1970s, the issue of race had caused black skaters to start picketing the games, forcing the teams to take sides. I personally believe this is what killed the Roller Derby.

MOBILE GAS-STATION ATTENDANT

When Francine and I got married, I had been a carpenter, and while in college at Emporia State, I was a clothier, gas-station attendant, half-assed mechanic, and general jack-of-all-trades. When we returned from Reno after getting married, I tried getting my old carpenter's job back, but it was November, and that usually meant little work opportunity. I called my old friend Wayne Campbell, who had let me work on weekends at his Mobile gas station at the corner of Jackson and Calaroga Avenues in Hayward, California. Back then, he had a great following at his station. It was the last station before the San Mateo Bridge and the first available station once you got off the bridge. The station was open twenty-four hours a day to help motorists with bad wiper blades, flat tires, loose radiator hoses, and other problems, as well as to provide gasoline.

I had to catch a cab in the early morning to arrive at the station by six o'clock in order to take over for the night shift. There were no buses going that way so early. At midnight, when I got off after my long shift, I took a bus to downtown Hayward and transferred to another bus that passed the Nimitz Motel, where we were living. Poor Francine was alone for those eighteen-hour days in our little kitchenette with nothing but the small TV to keep her company. I, on the other hand, had gas to pump, dirty windshields to clean, wiper blades to replace, tires to change, and oil and lube jobs to do in order to pass the time.

All the while, I was just waiting until the Roller Derby was ready to start up again.

During our five-month Bay Area schedule, I normally worked at the station on Saturdays until I had to drive to a game. During the week, I worked as a carpenter, and I would leave my job early to pick up Francine and drive to our next venue in Santa Rosa, San Jose, Monterey, or wherever we were playing. I know now why my body is worn out.

Wayne moved home to Ada, Oklahoma, when the state took over his land to expand the freeway. He opened a successful service station there.

DAYS OFF AND THE MOVIES

When on the road, our days off were filled with sleep, football, baseball, volleyball, barbecues at the closest park, and movies at night, followed by poker games. We always tried to keep current with the best movies. When we found one we thought we would like, it was not uncommon for a group of us to go together. As a matter of fact, it became the in thing to do. First, a few of us would see a film, and then we would act out some of the scenes with dialogue from the movie. Then others in the dressing room would decide to go. The next day off, more people would go to see the movie, and before long, we were recounting most of the dialogue and certainly the jokes and punch lines.

The Sound of Music really struck a chord with us—pun intended. The gay boys soon learned all the songs, and they would break into song with little prodding. That particular movie had a lot of songs that everyone loved to sing. For months, we sang the score of *The Sound of Music* over and over again.

Another all-time favorite was *Blazing Saddles*. The bad jokes and the bean-eating scene around the campfire were always reasons for someone to start reenacting a scene if someone farted in the dressing room. For some reason, everyone in the men's dressing room had to have contests for the best fart. Before long, we were naming them: fizz, fuzz, poop, fizzy fuzz poop, tear ass, rattler, atomic fallout, and electrical with juice. I know this all sounds childish, and it was, but it made us laugh, and we all had a great time.

The all-time favorite was *It's a Mad, Mad, Mad, Mad World*, which garnered the most reaction over the years. The main scene consists of a long food fight—something that really worked for us. It all started about the time when Jerry Seltzer starting having steak dinners for all the skaters on our nights off. We were selling out everywhere, and people started talking about getting raises. Jerry headed this off by providing steak dinners on our nights off. We would all head into a private dining room at the hotel and have a great meal complete with salad, baked potatoes, big steaks, and dessert. Our drinks were limited to coffee, iced tea, or soda. That lasted for only one night, and then we all started at the bar and had drinks sent to our tables. That was when the fun began. After seeing that movie, a few of the skaters decided to start throwing food at each other. Before long, we had a full-blown food fight. The night-off dinners ended after only a few weeks because of our bad behavior. Raises happened only for those willing to take Jerry on.

DEEP-SEA FISHING
AND BARBECUE

In 1969, we were kicking butt all over the United States. Every arena we played was sold out and packed to the rafters. We split the San Francisco Bay Area Bombers into two road teams: the San Francisco Bay Bombers and the Oakland Bay Area Bombers. Francine and I were with the Oakland team, along with Joan Weston, the ladies' captain, and Ken Monte as head coach. Yes, I said Ken Monte. It's funny when someone as disliked as Ken Monte, who was hated for his brutal skating tactics, suddenly puts on a Bomber uniform and is loved instantly by all of those fans.

We were skating sixteen to seventeen days in a row before a day off. Then we would have a 1,200- to 1,400-mile road trip. We were in Atlanta, Georgia, and were scheduled to skate in Mobile, Alabama, in two days. Since we would be at the coast, we planned a beach party, deep-sea fishing trip, and barbecue in Pensacola, Florida, on our way to Mobile. Mike Gammon; his wife, Judy McGuire; Dave Cannella; John Early; Barbara Baker; Bobby Jennings; and a few other skaters were all part of the group. We met at a beach in Pensacola to buy snorkeling gear, mats for floating, two hibachi grills, and steaks the size of the grills. We rounded out our picnic with potato salad, chips, beer, wine, watermelon, and dessert.

It was about two o'clock in the afternoon when we got to the beach. It took us about an hour to make our purchases, making it almost three o'clock by the time we were snorkeling and body surfing. The visibility in the water was terrible; even Monterey Bay in California was better than this. But here we were, thousands of miles from home, weary from all the games, driving, and hotel stays, and we were craving some good old California beach barbecue. I had recently bought a Super 8 movie camera, and I filmed this great day in the sun on the beach, with all of us around the campfire under the stars, singing, laughing, and telling bad jokes. I don't know if it was the booze or just the good times, but we were all so happy that we were acting as if this were our first barbecue on the beach.

Around midnight, we packed up and finished our trip to Mobile. We were tired and sleepy but happy. The game in Mobile was fantastic. We all had a new lease on life. We laughed, joked, and enjoyed skating again. The fans responded with cheers and laughter as we performed. Our next day off was in Corpus Christi, Texas, and more of the skaters wanted what we had found—bliss.

In Corpus Christi, we booked a deep-sea fishing boat trip at five o'clock in the morning. It turned out that the deep-sea fishing trip was not so deep. They took us out in the shallow bay, and that was as deep as we got. Barbara Baker caught the first and biggest fish, winning all the money in the pot. Joanie Weston caught a drumfish and a couple of sea bass. With all the fish caught among the skaters, we had enough for a fish fry. I almost caught a stingray. As I was reeling it in, one of the crew cut my line. I watched as the stingray slipped back into the bay. Stingrays were protected, and you could be fined if you brought one of them on board.

When we got back to the hotel, Joanie asked the head chef to cook up our fish and add vegetables, salad, and french fries to our meal, which we invited him and his crew to share in. He fixed the best fish fry any of us had ever had. The beer and wine flowed, and the fish tales grew as we drank, ate, and told our fish stories. My stingray became a four-foot shark, and the drumfish that got away was as big as a porpoise.

We started making plans on our days off. We would take over a local park with our hibachi grills, volleyball nets, and basketball and baseball games, even in the snow. Many times, the local police would check us out, because we were a motley crew. The police would drive by and see a group of hippie-looking girls and bearded men in the park with our barbecues going and loud music and a volleyball, basketball, or baseball game going on. We would be laughing, and we guessed they thought we must be on drugs.

Usually, by the time we were done, some of the police officers would participate in the games with us. Later, we would see them at the Roller Derby game with their families, and they'd ask us to pose with them and their families, which we would happily do. This was a great time in America and a great time for our sport. We were having fun on the road. Barriers were coming down, and lifetime friendships were made. It was a great life and a great time. Today I look back on these times and thank God for keeping us safe and giving us that opportunity.

DAVE CANNELLA AND ME IN MARS

In 1964, Dave Cannella, a rookie from Indianapolis, and I were roommates, and we once had two days off in Mars, Pennsylvania, a small town about forty or fifty miles outside of Pittsburgh. Dave had been married and had two kids, but tragedy had struck one Saturday night as Dave finished dirt-track racing a few hundred miles from his home. His wife was in the family car, and she left the track a few minutes ahead of Dave. He was in his pickup, pulling a trailer carrying his race car. Just ahead, he could see flames and red lights flashing from police cars, and a cold, chilling feeling came over him as he wondered if his family was involved in the accident. As he got closer, he recognized the car and saw it was engulfed in flames with all his dreams inside. He never spoke of the details, but apparently, a drunk driver in a semitruck had run a red light and broadsided the car with his family inside. It had burst into flames almost instantly, and they did not have a chance to escape.

Dave spent a couple of years inside a bottle. Only the dream of skating in the Roller Derby brought him out. He convinced Ken Monte to let him try out without going through a training center first. Needless to say, he was raw as a skater, and in a few weeks, he was offered a job as a referee and truck driver since he had a class-A license and experience driving an eighteen-wheeler. He didn't have the training and skill to be a skater. Something he always wanted was to skate, even more than car racing. While in Mars, Dave rebuilt the engine of his Pontiac Lemans, and I helped him. I had worked at a gas station during college; plus, my dad was always rebuilding cars, even if they didn't need it. After we got the car running, we decided to go horseback riding. Dave talked to the motel manager and arranged for four of us to go horseback riding. The manager left out the part about how it would be with English saddles. I had only ridden with Western saddles, and I wasn't good at that. We rode for almost three hours up and down hills and plateaus and through brush and scrub trees, doing our best to hang on. You see, with English saddles, there are no saddle horns to keep you from sliding up around the neck of the horse. You have to squeeze your legs together and dig into the horse's sides to stay upright and in the saddle.

After we dismounted and stretched our legs, we needed to go into town to have a few—okay, a lot of—drinks. We stayed out till almost dawn, which was a bad move since we had to set up the track at ten o'clock in the morning and then skate that night at eight. The Pittsburgh Arena was cool. It was one of the first buildings I had seen with a roof that opened and allowed you to enjoy the summer weather. Unfortunately, it was January and cold outside, so there would be no open-air skating this time.

By the time the game started, not only were we hungover and tired, but also, our legs were tired and beginning to stiffen up, making skating a real effort. Poor Dave fell twice during warm-ups, and the girls were having trouble too. Our coach, Bert Wall, heard what we had done with our time off, so he decided to have a little fun. He made Dave and me skate as jammers, alternating as blockers, with no breaks in between. After the first half, Dave and I found a beer vendor who sold us a couple of beers. Boy, we needed it! In the second half, Bert took a little pity on us and let Dave block and allowed me to participate in every other jam. Thank goodness he took pity on us, or we would never have made it through the whole game.

After the game, we had to tear down the track and head to our next venue. I don't remember which town was next, only that it took us six hours to drive there. By the time we checked in and got a few hours of sleep, the four of us could barely walk. The horse ride had done us in more than the drinking. I believe we had twelve or thirteen games in a row before our next day off. We slept for the whole day and didn't plan on any more horseback riding.

Dave became one of our best referees and the best truck driver. He later married Lynn Batouluchi, a skater from New York. When we retired, Dave and Lynn lived with Francine and me for a few weeks while he and Lynn got on their feet financially. They later bought a home in Alameda, California, and a sailboat that Dave rebuilt. A couple of years later, they moved back east, and I lost track of them. A couple of years ago, I heard that Dave had passed away while living in Florida. Dave loved to scuba dive. He was the one who got me interested in diving and underwater photography. I will always remember how, even though he had to deal with so much sorrow, Dave finally moved on and rebuilt his life. I look forward to seeing him again when God takes me home.

JO JO STAFFORD

Today I learned that Jo Jo Stafford passed away. I missed his funeral while I was attending the funeral of a family member in Ohio. I will always regret not taking the time to reconnect with him. A couple of months ago, an orderly at Kaiser Hospital in Walnut Creek told me that Jo Jo had come in for treatment in Fairfield or Sacramento, but he wasn't sure which one. That same orderly told me of the work Jo Jo had done in helping his son and others in their pursuit of track careers. We both talked about Jo Jo's generosity and willingness to help others. I shared skating memories with him. Jo Jo was always a good skater and a great teammate. He was fine with not being in the limelight and enjoyed helping others to do better. He was always willing to help the new kids learn how to skate our game and do a better job.

I went to Ohio and the Cincinnati Gardens a while back to show Diane where we skated with the Ohio Jolters. While we were there, one of the building managers took us up to a fifty-year memorial they had put together of all the events that had taken place in the Gardens. Roller Derby had a prominent place in the display. I promised to send him more pictures and info for their display. I enclosed a copy of the team picture for the 1972 Ohio Jolters, which included number 7, Jo Jo.

He was a good man and friend. He will be missed.

God bless you and your family, Jo Jo.

LAST NIGHT IN MADISON SQUARE GARDEN

In 1965, the old, famous Madison Square Garden of New York City closed. Imagine, if you can, all the great athletic events, circus performances, concerts, and other events that got their start there. Playing the Garden was the best! If the New York City Garden crowd witnessed your fight, act, or skills, you had arrived. You were in. That was it. You couldn't find a bigger, more-important venue to perform in. And there we were, the Roller Derby, as the closing act. As a rookie skater, I didn't realize until years later how important that night was. Since that was my first time in New York, I thought there was always a large gathering of the press and wannabe skaters in the dressing room. It was a regular circus, or it seemed that way.

Before the game, it seemed every newspaper columnist in the state was interviewing us. For some reason, the media thought it a novelty that I was a rookie skating in the final game at the Garden. As I remember, Bob Woodbury of the Cardinals thought this was a perfect time to kick the crap out of the new kid, which was me. Every time I tried to score, Bob would kick his right skate into my groin. Ouch! If I tried getting by him on the inside, which is not recommended and seldom successful, he would run me into the trainer's table in the infield. Finally, Charlie O'Connell dropped back and gave me one of the strongest whips I had ever had. I went flying down the straightaway toward Bob Woodbury. Just as he was getting set to block me, I noticed he had taken a wider stance so that he could really knock me down or out. I had seen my next move done by the ladies and thought, *Why not?* I kept up my speed, squatted, and flew through his legs, and just for payback, I used my hands to pull his skates out from under him. He went crashing down. The other skaters on the Pioneers blocked the Cardinal skaters up toward the rail, and I took the inside path in the turn and scored a grand slam—five full points—which won the game for us in the dwindling seconds on the game clock. I have never heard that much noise before. The fans were yelling, clapping, and jumping in the stands. We could feel the building shake. I thought we were having an earthquake.

Needless to say, I was the happiest kid in the world. Not only had we won the game, but also, I had scored the winning points with the help of my teammates. We would leave the Garden as the winning team in the last event to play the Garden. The next day, right there on the front page of the *New York Times* was Bob Woodbury with his arm around the neck of the rookie who would later score the winning points to close out the final event in the Garden. That was the first time I'd wanted to cut out a press clipping and send it home.

The next time we came to New York, we were skating in the new Madison Square Garden. The new building was, for its time, one of the finest sporting venues we would play. The Garden always made me feel special. The game and the energy were always a little greater, but for me, there was nothing like the old Garden.

MY LOST FINGER

Previously, I wrote about Dave Cannella's finger loss, and now I will tell about the loss of part of the index finger on my left hand. It was 1967, and Francine and I were skating for the Bay Bombers. It was late in the season, close to the play-offs and our fall break. We had planned to do some diving trips in Northern California and visit family during our ten-week break. It was a typical Monday night in San Jose. We always played Monday nights in San Jose. This was before Monday Night Football had secured Monday nights.

We were skating against Ronnie Robinson and the New England Braves. In the men's sixth period, Ronnie was kicking the crap out of me, as usual, and I was trying to protect myself, when I decided I'd had enough. He knocked me down next to the high part of the track, against the kick rail. He was trying to kick me off the track into the seating area. My job was to take it and then get revenge in the last period, but I had had enough. His last kick to my groin made me see red. I grabbed his skate and started twisting it and his leg until he fell onto the track. Because of the height of the track in that area, he slid down toward the infield, which allowed him to slip my grip and get back onto his skates. By that time, I was up on my skates, chasing him in the opposite skating direction with the referees after the both of us.

Ronnie could run well. I was closing in on him, when he suddenly went straight toward the infield and the penalty box, where he belonged. As he went by the penalty box, he grabbed it to slow himself down and to escape my outstretched hand. The penalty box was made of three pieces of plywood held together with hinges on the back piece and the two sides. The box was made of half-inch plywood; the back was four by three feet, and the two sides were two feet long and three feet high. Its weight was about thirty pounds. As Ronnie grabbed the box, it started to fall—with my index finger caught in between the back and one of the sides. As the box fell, it pinched the end of my index finger off.

The pain was instant, and I knew what had happened, but I still went for Ronnie. As I caught him, I hit him as hard as I could, but the boxing training his dad, the great Sugar Ray Robinson, had given him caused my punch to only graze the side of his jaw. Even though it knocked him down, it wasn't enough to put him out. By now, the pain in my hand was getting worse, and the other skaters near me saw the tip of my finger on the track. They were going crazy, saying my whole finger had been pinched off. It was only taken off to the first joint. Referees and the trainer were at my side, and someone wrapped up my bleeding hand in a towel. They escorted me off the track to the dressing room to wait for the ambulance that would take me to the hospital.

As hard as it might be to believe, my surgeon was named Dr. Hand. Really! He proposed doing a new procedure called a cross-finger flap. It involved cutting a large section from the top of my middle finger and sewing it onto the missing portion of my index finger. The two fingers would stay attached for seven to eight weeks, and then he would cut the flap and separate my fingers. It would be another four to five weeks before I could expect to have some degree of normalcy. Unfortunately, I usually worked as a journeyman carpenter during the off-season, and there was no way for me to do anything as physical as carpentry with my injury.

To make matters worse, I was only an ocean check away from receiving my NAUI (National Association of Underwater Instructors) scuba diver certification. So for the final dive, I took an average plastic garbage bag and wrapped up my hand. Now, keep in mind that I had sterile wrapping around my hand, making it the size of two softballs. The sterile wrapping and the garbage bag created a large bundle for my left hand. When we got to Monterey for our scuba checkout, all my fellow divers knew what I was trying to do. One of the other divers had been at the game and had already told them about the surgery. The dive instructor was reluctant to let me try to dive. He was worried not only about the sheer size of the dressing but also about seawater getting into my wound and causing an infection. I assured him that the bag would keep my hand dry. I told him the doctor had given me permission to dive. That was not true.

The big ball of gauze on my hand became a real problem. First, it was buoyant, which made it hard for me to navigate and to keep out of the kelp beds. Second, when we exchanged masks on the ocean floor, I was clumsy and had a hard time equalizing the pressure in the mask and vacating the water from inside the mask. Last but not least, the bag leaked badly, allowing seawater to penetrate the sterile dressing. I knew the doctor would be upset when he found out. I realized I had made a poor decision, but I wanted to complete the certification. I couldn't make the second dive, so I did not get certified. Then I had to wait until the following year to complete my certification. I talked Cliff Butler into going through the certification with me, and we were certified together.

Before the drive home, I stopped at Fisherman's Wharf and took a shower, cleaning my hand up the best I could, but it was a mess and throbbing. It hurt. On Monday, I made an appointment with Dr. Hand. He took one look at my hand and gave me a real chewing out. In that short amount of time, my surgery had become infected, and he told me I might lose both fingers. He gave me instructions to clean the wound every couple of hours for the next week or two, and he told me it would be painful. I had to suction off the infected area, put an antibacterial liquid on it, and apply a clean dressing to the open wound. He scared me into believing him, and I did exactly what he told me to do. After a few weeks, he separated the two fingers. I did my part by cleaning and dressing the wound for the next three or four weeks. The fingers were mending well, and the wound was closing.

It took another four months before I could turn nails and risk using a hammer or saw again. Jerry Seltzer knew I needed money, as I was unable to work during the off-season and unable to work full-time on the track crew. He gave me another assignment: handling the sale of programs at each building. I would receive shipments from the West Coast and insert the team lineups, count the programs, and then assign them to the concession managers in the arenas. After the game, I would settle up with the concession managers, count the unsold programs, and make bank deposits as soon as possible in the next town. I still helped the track crew when I was able. I did start the new season with the other skaters and Francine. I didn't get to travel as much as we had planned during the off-season, but I have all my digits. The only problem is that my index finger now has hair growing out of the end, which I have to trim every couple of weeks. I did return to normal, and I have only a weird scar to show for that night I lost my finger.

CHARLIE O'CONNELL, JOAN WESTON, ANNE CALVELLO, BOB HEIN, AND MANY MORE

Maybe the title of this chapter should be the name of this book. There were only a couple of times in the United States when Francine and I made the marquee; otherwise, we were part of the "many more." In Canada, we were almost always the top billing. I know it shouldn't mean much, but the truth is—who wouldn't want to be on the marquee? That meant you had made it. You were the big cheese, and you got the best salary. After all, we were working to win the game, but skating was also our job. We wanted to be the best and be the skaters the crowds came to see.

Over the last seven years, I spent most of my spare time working on this collection of stories from the Roller Derby in the hopes that maybe it would be published—not only because of the historical value but also because no one has really written about the true life on the road and at home. In 1970, Frank De Ford of *Sports Illustrated* lived with us for six weeks, and he wrote a book about what he had observed. His book was great; I liked it. But his book was based on observations, whereas I'm coming from the perspective of someone who lived the life of a Roller Derby skater.

I placed my only copy of his book in my father's casket upon his death. He was so proud of that book and of knowing that his son had been mentioned. My father died in 1979, and it wasn't until my birthday in

2001 that I received another copy from my life partner, Diane Sass. She and my ex-wife planned a Roller Derby birthday party for me, and Diane searched the web, including eBay, until she located a copy of the book for sale in Sweden. She had gotten me the perfect gift. I had cold chills run down my spine when I opened that package. She also had some tapes of prior games that she had gotten off the Internet. She and I are in a committed relationship, and she and I work for Re/Max Accord Real Estate in Livermore, California. We hope to retire someday and take our motor home out on the road to visit some of the many places that are a part of my Roller Derby past. Now we can both experience this beautiful country we love. Francine and her husband, Steve, have similar goals.

PROMOS, RADIO, TV, AND NEWSPAPERS

Last night, I celebrated my daughter's thirtieth birthday with about twenty of her friends. While she was opening her gifts and we were eating cake, one of her friends asked me about the Roller Derby life and if we enjoyed being famous. I had to chuckle and explain to her that we hadn't felt famous. The life on the road was the worst, with five or six months of one-night stands followed by four-hundred- to five-hundred-mile trips in between the sixteen to seventeen nights in a row that we skated. Many times, before a day off, we had to travel anywhere from eight hundred to a thousand miles to our next destination.

She then asked about the radio shows and TV appearances my daughter had told her about. It made me think for a couple of moments about how Francine and I felt during the first few TV and radio appearances and about the newspaper articles we would sometimes get to read. Those made us feel special for about two seconds. First of all, Francine spoke little English when she started in the Roller Derby. She was born and raised in Montreal, Canada, and her native language was French. So having to appear on American TV, answer questions on the radio, or have a newspaper columnist ask her questions was uncomfortable for her. I had stuttered for most of my life. As it turned out, doing interviews was therapeutic for both of us.

Francine was a novelty. She was only four feet eleven, and she was skating with big women during a time when women's sports were just beginning to emerge. They always liked the story about how we met in Montreal—that story will be for another day. Jerry Seltzer liked to book us for interviews a little ahead of the team, which meant we would leave right after the game and drive all night to the next city in order to make a radio interview or TV spot in the early morning. We normally met with a newspaper reporter before the game.

I would leave poor Francine in the dark about the upcoming interviews, because the appearances made her so nervous. I would tell her as we pulled off the highway and onto a gravel road toward a small building with a radio tower that we were doing a show. When it was a newspaper story, I would head downtown to their office for the interview. When it came time for a TV spot, I would tell Francine early so that she could dress properly. I had made the mistake of not telling her before, and she was mad at me for some time.

The most fun we ever had was also the most nerve-racking experience. We were on a game show called *What's My Line?* It was recorded in the old Ed Sullivan Theater in New York. We skated in a game in Cincinnati and then flew into New York. We arrived at the hotel close to four o'clock in the morning, and we had to be at the theater at seven thirty for the taping. Francine didn't sleep at all, as she was so nervous, and she spent the time getting ready. I slept for about two hours and then ordered breakfast in our room.

This was in 1971, and Manhattan was a sea of yellow cabs when we went outside to catch a ride. I tipped the doorman, and in no time, he had a cab pulling up to take us the few blocks to the theater. When we got there, we met with a producer in a tiny room under the stage. He told us what to expect from the stars who would be asking us questions: Soupy Sales, Dorothy Kilgallen, and two others whose names I don't remember. One of the guys was married to the actress who played the mother on *The Partridge Family*. The producer told us that five shows would be taped that day, and he wasn't sure which show we would be on and wouldn't know until later. Good news! Bad news! Our show was taped last, at about three o'clock in the afternoon. We were so tired by then that we were numb. The good news is that we got to meet several of the stars. It was an exciting experience.

Francine did a great job. Everyone loved her. It turned out that Dorothy was a fan. She recognized us, and she recused herself. By the time the show was done, we were dead tired, but we still had to go over to the *New York Times* office for an interview, and at that time of day, catching a cab was impossible. So we walked the five or six blocks to their office, gave an interview, and had some pictures taken to be released before our next game at Madison Square Garden.

Over the years, we had occasion to read some of the things written about us. I'll tell you—it was frustrating how they would twist what we had said or edit it in such a way as to change the meaning of what we had said. That lesson has remained with both of us in regard to giving interviews voluntarily. For several years, I was the public-relations chairperson for our board of Realtors, and I served on the California Association's state committee, so I had to give interviews every now and then. Because of my past experiences, to this day, I take all news reporting with a grain of salt.

We didn't feel famous, but when asked, we still sign autographs and are happy to talk about our glory days in the Roller Derby.

ROOKIE IN NORFOLK, VIRGINIA

In the winter of 1964, as a rookie, I was introduced to the real life as a stranger in Norfolk, Virginia, when I had a couple of days off from the Roller Derby. I was introduced to pedicures, manicures, navy-style haircuts, and raw oysters by the tub with lots of beer.

We had been on the road for a few weeks with little time off. Boy, were we all ready to relax, party, and recharge our batteries. The team arrived at our hotel in downtown Norfolk, and it looked like something out of a horror movie. Really! It was an old Victorian-style hotel with about five or six stories and a see-through wrought-iron elevator that reminded us of movies in which people were shot at through the grates; the elevator cable broke, sending the elevator plummeting to the basement floor; or the elevator got stuck between floors and then, as people tried to escape through the open doors, started up and cut them in half. Remember those movies? I certainly do. I walked up the stairs to the fifth floor instead of using that elevator. After all, I was a Roller Derby star—okay, a rookie. But a little exercise couldn't hurt, and I felt much safer.

Since I had been on the road for a few weeks, working construction, driving, and skating, I needed a haircut. I walked to the closest barbershop I could find. When I entered the shop, the owner's eyes started rolling up like a slot machine that stopped with dollar signs showing. I didn't notice at the time, but reflecting upon the events of the day with a few beers under my belt, I realized I had been set up.

The barber greeted me with a firm, friendly handshake and invited me to sit in his luxury barber chair. Immediately, two young, nice-looking ladies came over to help me feel welcome. While the barber murmured something in a southern drawl, with big, toothy smiles, his female assistances went to work on me: one was at my feet, taking off my shoes and socks and preparing for a pedicure, while the other immersed my hands in a dish with good-smelling soapy water. While they were working on my pedicure and manicure, the barber gave me a navy-style haircut (a buzz cut). Before they finished the pedicure and manicure, a third young lady came out of the back room and started to massage my neck and shoulders. Wow! I couldn't believe all the attention I was getting. Boy, what service! When I saw my haircut in the mirror, I almost fainted.

The barber saw my shocked face, and he began to talk to me about the bill I had run up with his toothy southern drawl. By the time he stopped speaking, I realized I had spent half a week's salary for a haircut, massage, pedicure, and manicure, when all I'd wanted was a little trim. Before I could get out of the chair, a guy who appeared to be about eight feet tall came from the back room and stood behind the barber as I worked to pull the money out of my pocket. I only had around thirty dollars (half a week's pay) on me at the time. Fortunately for me, we were getting paid later that day, so I would still have beer and food money, thank goodness. When I recounted my story at the pool to the gang, everyone had a good laugh at my expense. Keep in mind that young sailors from the navy were coming into town for a little action, and apparently, the barbershop was a front for the action, which took place in the back room, where all the young, lovely ladies had come from. Had I only known, I could have gotten a real trim.

Being raised in central California and having parents who were farm workers, as a twelve-year-old, I worked with my brother, sister, and parents in the fields. I had never even heard of raw oysters until I was in high school. The concept was something I couldn't grasp—why would someone pay to eat raw oysters? Have you ever seen those things? Yuck!

Make that double yuck! After having a few (a lot of) beers around the pool and telling the group about my fiasco with the barber, I was easily talked into trying some of the oysters. We had three washtubs full of oysters and bowls of Cajun hot sauce and ketchup to wash them down with. Wow! I was hooked.

I spent most of the next day in the bathroom with my face in the commode. Man, what a hangover! Finally, my roommate, Dave Cannella, convinced me to try the so-called hair of the dog, or more beer. Can you believe that? But it worked. After a few too many beers, I was feeling great, and by game time, I was back to my old self—well, almost. Either way, I had survived Norfolk, and I had learned not to nod my head or say yes until I fully understood what I was agreeing to. That lesson has stuck with me till this day.

SETTING UP AND TEARING DOWN THE ROLLER DERBY TRACK

One of the marvels of Roller Derby life was the process of track setup and teardown. When the game first started, there were no portable tracks, as each city we went to had a track of its own. In those days, the track was 120 feet long and 60 feet wide rail to rail. The actual skating-surface width was twelve feet and still is today.

When we started to use portable tracks and moved from city to city, the guys would pitch in and take the track apart and load it into a semitrailer for the trip to the next city. There the male skaters would spend between ten and fourteen hours putting the track back together. We would repeat that process again and again as we skated through the season.

In 1964, when I started skating, a ten-man crew normally took ten hours to set up and eight hours to tear down and pack the track into the truck. The record, set by my crew in Victoria Island, Vancouver, Canada, in 1973, was fifty-four minutes for setup and thirty-six minutes for teardown. We had a crew of six men and two women. How did we get to that point?

Through the efforts of Gil Orozco, Bill Morrissey, and a few skaters and crew members, we figured out how to build a smaller track, one that would fit into any high-school gym, thereby providing us with more potential venues. The new track was ninety feet long and fifty feet wide, with the same twelve-feet-wide skating area. We discovered that if we numbered the pieces of the track, the uprights, and the midbraces that supported the skating surfaces, the whole process would be streamlined. We designed new pads for the rails and uprights, which better protected skaters from serious injury. When you are skating thirty to thirty-five miles per hour and slam into a two-by-four rail padded with only a half inch of foam, there isn't a lot of flexibility, so your ribs and stomach take the brunt of the blow.

Next, we learned by watching other groups, such as the circus, bands, and stage shows, to see how they moved stuff in and out. At first, we used piano dollies, but after several accidents, we went for stage carts like those used to move scenery. With these carts, we could move the pieces from the truck into the buildings with the aid of a twenty-foot ramp extended from the back of the truck to the arena floor. We reduced the number of people needed to bring pieces in from the truck to the arena. With one person in the truck and one person manning a cart, we could easily load the two-hundred-pound track piece onto the cart and run the cart into the building, where it was immediately unloaded and attached to the preceding track piece. By the time the truck was fully unloaded, the track was nearly set up.

Underneath the track, one person would attach center bolts halfway down the length of the iron rails that framed each section of the track, or Dixies, as we called them. Another person would attach the midbraces that reinforced each midsection, and the center-bolt person would attach a brace from underneath the track. While this was going on, another crew member would screw down a piece of Masonite to create the smooth skating surface. While waiting for the next section to arrive, the crew would attach the top rails and pads. When the truck was empty, the track would be ready for the final safety check.

When it came time to take the track down, we reversed the process. The primary reason this process worked was threefold: First, we were guaranteed a five-hour setup wage and a three-hour teardown wage regardless of how long the job took. Next, each person learned how to do every part of the job, in case someone got hurt and his or her spot needed to be filled. Finally, everyone knew that when we finished the job, we could head to a bar or poker game or get a start on the next trip.

Many times, we received applause from the early crowds who came to watch the track-setup ballet. It was fascinating to watch. Often, new building managers would be terrified to discover that the track would not be set up until it was almost game time. However, after they saw the ballet, they were impressed. Because of the mobile track, we could follow an afternoon hockey game with the Roller Derby, increasing the revenue for the arenas. As soon as the hockey game, basketball game, or play was over, we could start laying out floor and setting up the track.

STOCKTON TO RENO TO FARGO

One of my fondest memories is the start of the 1969 Eastern season. Of course, I'm kidding. After a matinee game in Stockton, California, that ended around four o'clock in the afternoon, Francine, Bobby Jennings, and I headed for Reno, Nevada. We had to take the track down, eat dinner, and then start the 1969 Roller Derby road trip. By the time we got to Reno, which was about a four-hour drive, we were exhausted. After checking in to the hotel, we went straight to our rooms. Francine and I made the mistake of going back downstairs for a quick bite and a little gambling, while Bobby, being the smart one, went to sleep.

Those of you who know Francine understand that she loves to gamble—not just slot machines but real poker: seven-card stud. She and I gambled till dawn, and then we tried to grab a few hours of sleep. That day, in the early afternoon, Francine and I had a TV appearance on a local daytime talk show. We must have done fairly well, since the game was a sell-out, something we had not experienced in Reno for quite some time. The sales might not have been because of our special appearance on local TV, but it makes me feel better to believe that they were.

After the show, I dropped Francine off at the hotel to sleep. Yeah right! She gambled until it was time to leave for the game. I went to the arena to set up the track and hopefully get a catnap in the dressing room. Have you ever tried to sleep on a wooden bench in a room with eight other guys talking, laughing, and generally making noise? Well, I managed to get a little rest.

As I said earlier, the place was sold out, and we had a great game. I helped tear the track down after the game and repacked the car for our trip to Fargo, North Dakota. Keep in mind that it was January. We would be dealing with snow and ice while driving straight through to Fargo. Did I mention that neither Bobby nor Francine could drive? That's right—I drove straight through. I drank so much coffee and took so many NoDoz tablets that I couldn't have slept if I'd tried.

The trip itself was uneventful. We did run into snow and black ice just outside of Little America, Wyoming, a major truck stop with hundreds of semitrucks at a massive gas station, truck stop, and motel combo. It's like an oasis in the middle of nowhere.

The point of my telling this story is to show that as hard as we worked, we tried to fit in some fun, even at our own expense. We could have had a good night's sleep in Reno and left Reno earlier the next morning, but the competitive spirit ran over into our driving practices. The first ones into a new town got the street-level rooms, which meant they could park outside their room and not have to unload the car. Since the normal road trip lasted between 150 and 180 days, that luxury became a strong motivator for leaving the night before. Additionally, the traffic was lighter at night, and the cops would let you drive faster. The results were quicker trips, first-floor rooms, and the satisfaction of getting there first. What could be better?

In another segment, I will tell you of the 1966 road trip from Reno to Fargo with Donald Drewry and Ken Kunzelman in an El Camino loaded with Roller Derby programs. We faced black ice and spinouts, and we sometime drove at 110 miles per hour. We beat everyone by eleven hours.

THE SAMOA CONNECTION

Two of the Roller Derby's fiercest male opponents came from the island of Samoa. Sam Tiapula and Lia Mefie were both royalty in their home country. They both had large families in the Bay Area who frequently attended the home games. They let everyone know who they were rooting for. Sometimes their families would do war chants to encourage the skaters. When they were skating against one another, fights would break out between family members.

On the road, Sam worked on the track crew, and boy, he was a good worker. He never allowed the track work to slow him down in the game. When Sam gave you a block, he almost always caused your bones to ache because he hit so hard. Lia wasn't as agile as Sam on the track, but he was taller and knew how to use height to leverage a block. Either way, when I saw the Samoan Express coming, I either quickened my pace or set myself up for a hard hit.

Off the track, the two young warriors practiced the Samoan sword dance in their hotel room, causing many a maid to run for the hills. Sam explained to me one day that he and Lia had to demonstrate their ability to do the ancient dance so that they could pass it on to their male children. It was expected. A couple of times, they even practiced the fire dance outside on the lawn of the Holiday Inn. That stopped quite a few cars and spectators in their tracks. Onlookers were surprised by the show the boys put on.

Someday I would like to go to Samoa and see the beautiful island the boys described as their true home. Magazine articles and travel videos don't do it justice, according to Sam. Over time, I learned to trust him—he never lied to me.

TRADING BEER AND SODAS FOR MY FIRST HOME

When I agreed to start selling beer and sodas to the teams after the game, I didn't realize the job would earn me the money for the down payment on my first home. That is exactly what happened. Normally, a beer vendor would come into our dressing room after a game and sell us beer and sodas. That tradition was sacred for our home games in the Bay Area. On the road, vendors seldom, if ever, ventured into our dressing room. Since I was known to be enterprising and responsible, I was asked to ice down chests of beer and soda for the men's and women's dressing rooms. Every week or so, I purchased several cases of beer and soda and stored them in the truck, along with our programs.

In some states, I had to shop at state liquor stores, while in others, I went to the local supermarket. Because of the low prices in those days, I charged fifty cents for a soda and a buck for a beer, which might seem low now, but back then, it afforded me a small profit. After a lengthy road trip, I was often amazed at the amount of money I had saved. In four years, I saved enough for Francine and me to make the down payment on our first home. It was a modest, older fixer-upper selling for $31,500. That was a lot of money in 1970. Our first house payment was $265 per month, including taxes.

HAWAII OR OUR FIRST HOME—WE HAD TO CHOOSE

That first home replaced my dream of a trip to Hawaii. Francine was adamant that we buy a house first. We could go to Hawaii later. As it turned out, we went to Hawaii in 1979, several years after we left the Roller Derby. But she was right; the house was a great investment for us. Later, we purchased property in Maui, Hawaii, and visited the island several times a year.

WHAT'S MY LINE?

I believe it was the winter of 1971 when Francine and I received word that we would be appearing on the television show *What's My Line?* Fortunately for us, we had done many TV interviews, radio interviews, and other media events. But we were both a little nervous about taping a show with great ratings before a live audience and nationwide viewership of millions every week. I should point out here that Francine is French Canadian, and English was her second language. The news of an upcoming interview sent her weeping into the restroom, telling me what she really thought about this aspect of our career. Only God knows what else she told me, since she would often berate me in her native tongue, French.

As the time drew near for our trip to New York, we realized we would be flying in after a game in Atlanta and arriving in New York at about one o'clock in the morning. We would need to grab a taxi into Manhattan, check in, and be at the Ed Sullivan Theater by seven thirty. The game in Atlanta was a tough one for Francine. Though she did her best skating, Jan Vallow knocked her all over the place. Ann Calvello, our girls' captain, did everything she could to protect Francine, but she was beaten up pretty badly.

It was two thirty in the morning by the time we arrived and got our room—or should I say our hotel closet. The room was so small that we had to practically climb over the bed just to get into the room, and this was the Waldorf. As I said, we had to be at the Ed Sullivan Theater by seven thirty. According to the doorman, while the theater was just a few blocks away, it was a thirty-minute cab ride because of the amount of traffic. Being a guy, I brushed my teeth and headed to bed. Francine, on the other hand, spent the rest of the early-morning hours getting ready for the show. I don't think she got two hours of sleep before we had to leave for the show.

When morning came, we headed downstairs, where the doorman hailed a cab to take us to the theater. The trip really did take all of thirty minutes. We were happy we had allowed the extra time. I don't remember the producer's name, but he and his assistant greeted us, got us coffee and bagels, and told us to have a seat backstage. He explained the format of the show and took us downstairs for a practice question-and-answer period. I should point out that Francine had never seen or heard of the show, even though it was popular in Canada.

While sitting backstage, we were able to watch the taping of the shows ahead of us. They taped five shows in one day, and the shows would air daily during the upcoming week. We weren't told that ours was the last show of the day to be taped, so we sat and sat, drinking too much coffee, until three o'clock rolled around, when it was time to tape our show. Had we known we would be sitting for so long, we would have stayed at the hotel, gotten some sleep, and been at the theater in plenty of time for our taping. The good news is that we got to meet all the stars who appeared on the show: Soupy Sales, Dorothy Kilgallen, Sid Cerise, Carol Channing, Gig Young, Elia Kazan, and others whose names I have forgotten.

When our time came, the master of ceremonies sat us at a table onstage. The four stars who would be asking us questions sat at a table across from us. We had some adoring fans watching from the audience. The format was simple: the stars took turns asking us questions about our lives without actually asking what we did for a career. Dorothy Kilgallen had to excuse herself since she was a fan of the Roller Derby and instantly knew who we were. The other stars on the panel kept trying to get her to give them hints. We were successful. They were unable to guess our occupation. We were awarded a prize of $250 as well as some parting gifts: two sets of earrings, a necklace, and some perfume. I wanted to know why I didn't get some power tools or wrenches. All the prizes were for women. Talk about chauvinism!

When the taping was complete, we said our good-byes to our adoring fans. As we were leaving the building, we found ourselves looking at a sea of yellow cabs. What a sight! We needed to go to the *New York Times* office for an interview with one of their sports columnists. It took half an hour just to get a cab and travel about two blocks. Had we known the exact location, we could have walked there faster.

The interview was short, thank God. We helped the photographer identify some of the players in photos he had taken at the last game we'd played at the Garden. After the interview, we returned to the hotel. When we got back to our closet—or room, if you could call it that—we took a short nap before going down to the Market Basket restaurant for one of the best meals we had ever had. Since we were on an expense account, we had chateaubriand and a real Caesar salad prepared right at our table from scratch, and we topped off the wonderful meal with cherries jubilee and a bottle of cabernet sauvignon. What a meal!

The next day, we slept in until late morning, caught a cab to Kennedy Airport, and flew out to meet up with the team in Cincinnati. Eight weeks later, our show aired on TV, but we missed it because we were skating in Sacramento that night. This happened well before VCRs and DVRs, but our fans who saw it told us they thought it was cool that we were on the show. We did too.

THE KEZAR RIOTS

In 1964, I skated my first game at Kezar Pavilion in San Francisco, which was only three blocks from the corner of Haight and Ashbury. If those street names sound familiar, it is because of the worldwide notoriety they gained in the '60s. That location was known for hippies, drugs, and free love. It seemed as if a lot of trouble emanated from that neighborhood. The pavilion at Kezar was across the parking lot from the football stadium, where many football games were played, both professional and amateur. The stadium and pavilion backed up to the east end of Golden Gate Park, another hippie hangout. It was a wild place any time of day or night.

This was the site of our televised games, which were taped and sent all over the United States and Canada. The arena was ideal. The derby track fit inside the small arena as if it had been built specifically for it. The fans were only eight to ten feet away from the track, and most seats had a good view. As sometimes happens, a fight broke out on the track when a spectator's view was impaired by a pole. With his or her view blocked, the spectator would crowd into someone else's space, causing that person's view to be blocked, which resulted in some shouting and sometimes a fight between the fans, which we loved to watch.

Because the fans were so close to the track and we were on the main floor, surrounded by them, our only option during the fights was to get to the safety of our dressing rooms. This was fine if you wore the Bay Bomber uniform. If you were the visiting team, you risked life and limb trying to leave the track by navigating the slippery stairway to the dressing room. Normally, arena guards would form a safety path for us, but if a riot was going on, they were often too busy controlling the fans to worry about the skaters.

If my memory serves me well, many times, I witnessed the San Francisco riot police coming in to break up a fan-induced riot. Most of the time, they were called in when angry, drunk, or drugged fans surrounded the track and wouldn't let the skaters off. They wanted to kill someone for some infraction that a visiting team member had committed against one of their favorite skaters.

Sometimes the fans would charge the track and climb onto it with the skaters. This was a dumb move on their part. The standing rule in skating was to charge any fans who tried to get onto the track and to physically remove them, whether by severely kicking them, hitting them, or throwing them from the track. This might sound awful if you were a Bombers fan. The opposing teams loved to tussle with fans who made their way onto the track. They had vengeance on their minds and mayhem in their blood. I am not proud to say how many fans I slugged, kicked, or used a judo throw on in order to gain control of them before they injured a skater or themselves.

One Sunday-night game, when the great Ann Calvello was in her prime, she accepted some brownies from a fan and shared them with the other girls in the dressing room before the game. The brownies were laced with marijuana, and a short time later, the girls begin to get really weird. The game was going well enough, with lots of energy and mayhem. I think TV inspired many skaters to top their best performances. The girls started getting out of hand, and the guys' game was getting brutal. Ken Monte of the Red Devils was kicking the crap out of Charlie O'Connell, Tony Roman, and me. I think he might have been a bit intoxicated. The fans decided they needed to help us out, and the girls were encouraging them. Someone called for the riot police, who had a substation located in the back of the arena. They were in the arena within a couple of minutes. They came prepared with German shepherd police dogs and billy clubs, swinging at anyone out of his or her seat. If you were unlucky enough to be next to the track, you got your head cracked open. That night, they sent half a dozen people to the hospital.

The fans had gone too far, and the skaters had helped them. A member of my church was there, and he had his skull split open by the police before being arrested. When I saw him at church a few years ago, we had a good talk about what happened to him. He was prosecuted and served a month in jail after he got out of the hospital. Now, don't feel too bad for him, because he was one of the fans who tried to trip skaters as they came around the track. He hid behind other fans when they charged the track and reached out to grab a skater's ankle or leg, causing the person to trip. After his arrest, he sat in his seat and yelled but never again came up to the track during a game.

I will always remember Kezar Pavilion—the noise, the fans, the hippies from down the street, and all the wild times we had.

SAN JOSE MEMORIAL PARK RIOTS

Over my skating career, from late 1963 through 1974, I saw a lot of riots at our games. I have already written about Kezar Pavilion, and after this little story, I'll include the Chicago and Baltimore riots as well. Over the years, the pattern was the same: the visiting team would start a fight with one of our stars, and before long, they would enlist some of their cohorts to help injure the skater who was the crowd's favorite that night. The visiting players used punching, kicking, and general mayhem to injure our player. They never followed the rules while delivering their brand of punishment to the unlucky home-team skater. It always frustrated me when they hid this from the referees, until I found myself being the villain. It was actually simple to catch the referee looking at something else on the track as I punished another skater. Of course, the fans saw everything and were mad as hell at the referees. How could they have missed that punch or that kick to the groin? The referees did catch them occasionally and sent the offenders to the penalty box for two-minute time-outs.

In San Jose, California, we skated at the Memorial Stadium, a ball park with the track straddling first base, the pitcher's mound, and third base. This was all well and good for the promoter, but for the skaters, when we were knocked into the dirt and grass infield going between twenty-five and thirty miles per hour, it was unpleasant. Skaters tended to stop quickly and usually headfirst into something hard. It was not a pretty picture. It took a lot of training to learn how to keep from killing yourself or another skater when you exited the track.

The referees were always good targets to run into to keep from falling down. This threat caused them be alert for incoming skaters and, in turn, take their eyes off the game. The fans always thought the referees were missing the skating plays on purpose, but it was really for their own survival. The fans got hot at the referees for failing to catch all the penalties that should have been served on any visiting skaters who had the guile to take advantage of this fact to deliver punishment to the hometown fan favorite.

A referee who knew how to make lemonade out of lemons was William "Bill" Morrissey. He would stand with his hands folded across his chest and stare at the crowd with a look that said, "I'm in charge, and if you don't like it, tough." He especially made Charlie O'Connell mad. The visiting teams knew this and would set up Charlie with all kinds of punching, kicking, and even choking when Morrissey's back was turned. Their moves were almost like wrestling tactics. When Bill turned around, the bad guys would do it all over again. This would go on throughout the game. Sometimes they would get caught and be sent to the penalty box. Generally, they would get away with it, and Morrissey would give the fans and Charlie that look.

Bill Morrissey was a lousy skater but one of the best referees in the game. In my career, I got to see Bill skate in a match race against Charlie O. on three occasions. All three times were in the packed San Francisco Cow Palace with standing-room-only crowds. The race would start with O'Connell knocking Bill down right at the starting line. When Bill got up, O'Connell would knock him down again and again. On every lap, as Charlie came around, he would knock the crap out of Bill, and the fans would go wild. The race invariably ended with Bill bleeding and nearly unconscious, being carted off the track. The fans yelled at the top of their lungs for Charlie O. One of the worse riots I have ever seen was in San Jose, California, a few weeks earlier.

It was a nice summer night at the stadium during a game between the Bombers and the New England Braves. Charlie O. was getting the crap kicked out of him by Bob Hine and Ronnie Robinson, and we all tried to help him. We were doing our best to win the game while helping Charlie. Morrissey missed a number of opportunities to penalize the two bad boys. Then, from out of nowhere, Ronnie Robinson slowed Charlie on the straightaway and blocked him so that he couldn't see Bob Hine coming at him full speed. Bob Hine jumped up into the air with his skates aimed at Charlie's midsection. As Ronnie Robinson held Charlie's arms so that he couldn't protect himself, the full force of Hine's skates hit Charlie in the stomach at about thirty miles per hour. We all heard the ribs break. Our whole team went after Robinson and Hine. Those two jumped off the track and headed for the dressing room.

This was a typical ball park, with the dressing rooms under the bleachers and little protection from the fans. Almost as if they had been fired out of a cannon, fans rushed the track and continued toward the dressing-room area. I don't know who made the call, but the police arrived a short time later. By that time, we were locked in the dressing rooms with fans blocking the exits. They were getting louder and louder. When fans riot, they go after everyone, including the home team. Don't ask me why.

In the dressing room, we could hear the fans in the parking lot just behind the dressing rooms. They were trying to get in through the windows as well as the two doors, which we had barricaded. As a husband whose wife was at the other end of the stadium, I was worried about Francine and the other girls, but we had no way of getting to them. Hal Janowitz, a former skater and now box-office manager, came in and told us the girls were fine. It appeared that the fans wanted Bill Morrissey, Bob Hine, and Ronnie Robinson, in that order.

Through the window, we could hear fans shouting that they had found Morrissey's car in the parking lot. We could hear them breaking the windows and kicking cars, and then we heard someone shout, "It's on fire! Get back! It's going to blow!"

We could smell smoke in the dressing room, and we were scared that an explosion might take out the back wall of the dressing room, sending flaming debris through the windows. By this time, the riot squad and firemen had arrived to put out the blazing car. About that time, we heard a man screaming, "That's my car! What are you doing to my car?" Bill gave a sigh of relief.

It took the police a full hour to get the crowd settled down, with most of them heading for home. The fire department put out the flames, and we all escorted Bill and his wife, Dee, safely home. The fans really got their money's worth that night.

ROLLER DERBY AT THE FAIR

Jerry Seltzer, the owner of the International Roller Derby League as well as the six teams that comprised the league, was a shrewd businessman. He knew how to and where to promote. In the San Francisco Bay Area, there were several county fairs during the summer, and the Roller Derby was a natural event for those venues. Usually, after the horse racing was completed, our track crew moved in to set up the derby track, centered at the finish line. The fairgrounds strategically erected their grandstands in such a manner that the finish line was positioned at the center of the racetrack grandstands. The racetrack consisted of dirt, horse manure, sawdust, and windblown debris from the fair.

Some of my favorite memories of the fair circuit come from the Santa Rosa County Fairgrounds, where the track was inside a building with a concrete floor and stands on both sides of the track. The setting was intimate because of the small size of the building. This venue could accommodate about 3,500 people—not a bad weekday gate. We would usually skate half a dozen games a year there and then move to an outside racetrack during the fair. The fans in Santa Rosa were among the best. They knew the skaters by name, and they understood the game. They were loud and generous. Francine and I always received gifts from the fans in Santa Rosa.

The Santa Rosa fair crowd was a little different because we had people come from outside the area who were new to the derby and its rules. They would sometimes get rowdy. During one fair game at the racetrack with the dirt and manure infield, the fans got angry at one of the visiting skaters. I think it was Buddy Atkinson Sr. He was throwing powder into the eyes of the home-team skaters as they came around the turn. He would snap a towel out at them with the powder concealed inside. The powder was plaster of paris, a white substance used to give traction on an otherwise-slick track. This stuff got into your eyes and burned like crazy. It would impair your vision momentarily, and usually, the skater hit with it would crash into the rail or go into the infield. Either way, it was not a good thing.

The fans got mad, and they started throwing beer bottles at the track. This was before stadiums outlawed bottles. Then they started throwing glass ashtrays that they had won on the midway. These were lethal. One of our female skaters, not involved in the fight, was standing in the infield, when she was hit with an ashtray. It cut open her head and knocked her out. We rushed her to the hospital with a concussion, and she required several stitches.

Another time, at the Alameda County Fair, one of the rookie skaters for the Bombers was hit with a beer bottle, causing him to crash into an upright at full speed. He broke his leg in several places, ending his Roller Derby career.

Even though the fans could get rowdy at the fairgrounds, our number-one concern was the dirt infields. Just imagine: you are skating at twenty-five to thirty miles per hour on a smooth surface, when suddenly, you are shoved or blocked into the infield. You try to run through sawdust, dirt, and horse crap in a desperate attempt to keep your balance while trying to slow yourself down. Many times, we just crashed and burned, going headfirst into the dust, dirt, and crap. Or we might actually make it across the infield, only to step onto the track doing five to ten miles per hour in front of the skating pack going twenty-five to thirty miles per hour. Needless to say, a crash would probably occur. Dirt infields led to many more injuries per game than a normal skating environment.

The fun part of skating at the county fairgrounds was the opportunity to attend the fair. We got to go to the fair and see the booths, displays, and wonderful gadgets being demonstrated and, of course, the midway full of carnie games and crazy rides. Let's not forget betting on the horse races and enjoying all the cold beer, hot dogs, cotton candy, and candy apples. God, I'm getting hungry just thinking about it.

Games at the fair were different: we had to watch out for drunken fans and soft infields. But we had fun too. Many spectators who had never experienced a Roller Derby match before became fans. I told you Jerry Seltzer was a genius.

BALTIMORE RIOTS

In 1973, after being sold to Bill Griffith's Roller Games Derby, Francine and I were skating for the new Chicago Pioneers, which was my first Derby team. However, skating for the Roller Games was not the same as the International Roller Derby League. Roller Games was like wrestling on wheels. The plays and final outcomes were always set, and the fighting and mayhem were over the top. Don't get me wrong—the IRDL staged fights and plays, but we always were trying to win. There was a distinct line between skating and the show that was Roller Games.

During the time we worked for Roller Games, we had a game in Baltimore. We had heard stories of the riots and how Baltimore had a chain-link fence around its ice-hockey-style arena, with a wire tunnel that we'd have to skate through in order to get to the track. We were warned about the beer and soda bottles that would be thrown, and the language used would make a sailor blush. But nothing prepared us for the reality of the moment. I couldn't believe that civilized people could act that way. It was not something the families in the audience should have had to be around.

When we arrived at the track, all was quiet because we were early. The fans were just beginning to enter the building, and the energy in the air was growing. I went down to the track through the chain-link cage built around it, and it reminded me of the movie *Rollerball*, starring James Caan, set in the mid-twentieth century, a movie Francine and I had declined to work on, since it would have taken us to Germany for two months during the regular season. Francine and I were on the Canadian

All Stars, touring Canada coast to coast. This was Francine's dream. I recently watched *Rollerball* on HBO. It took me back to Baltimore and all the memories of our friends who skated in the movie. Some of the stories they told me about their time in Germany were hilarious and lucrative. They received more than $300 each time they took a fall. That was more than we were making in a week.

By the time warm-ups started, the fans had filled the building, and the noise level was intense. The yelling, shouting, and stomping made our dressing room shake. As we skated out through the chain-link-fence tunnel, the crowd pelted us with sodas, beer, and God only knows what else. The obscenities they used were creative, and I learned some new phrases that night. After warm-ups, as the visiting team, we would normally have gone back to the dressing room while the home team warmed up, but this time, it was safer for us to stay in the track's infield.

The fans went wild as their home team came out through the tunnel and entered the track. The fans were yelling and screaming for their team, using a lot of profanity. Their behavior was hard for this poor California boy to understand. When the game started, it seemed to me that the plays were too intense for this crowd. I knew they would probably start a riot. Sure enough, by halftime, the intensity had increased to a dangerous level. Buddy Atkinson threw plaster of paris into a hometown girl's face, causing her to fall.

In the next few seconds, it seemed as if hundreds of fans were rushing the track. We didn't feel safe with the limited protection of the chain-link-fence cover. The fans began tearing at the wires that held the fencing to the surrounding poles. In little time, the fencing started to come loose, which made it possible for a few hearty fans to enter the track. At that point, we were told to go to the dressing rooms and lock the doors. The riot squad had been called, but it took ten minutes or more for them to arrive and get some control over the situation. In the meantime, we were holding the dressing-room doors shut. The guards from the arena were outside the doors, trying to calm the fans.

We finally got a call telling us to go to a U-Haul truck waiting for us just outside the dressing-room doors. Someone had obtained an enclosed moving truck for us to use in our escape. An hour later, we were let out of the truck and allowed to go onto our team bus for the ride back to Philly.

Riots are more common than the average person would believe. Fans, when heated up by manipulation of an otherwise-sportsmanlike game, can erupt anytime and anywhere. After that game, I watched in awe European soccer matches and the ensuing riots. I thank God that our riots have not caused a single death, only a few injuries. We need to ask ourselves, "Is this really worth it?"

EVEL KNIEVEL IN LONG ISLAND, OR HOW TO GET DRUNK IN ONE EASY LESSON

Late in 1972, while we were booked at the Nassau Coliseum in Long Island, New York, we had the pleasure of drinking with none other than the great Evel Knievel. As it turned out, he was booked at the same hotel across from the coliseum.

No one in our group had ever seen him perform live, but we all knew his reputation and had seen his performances on TV. He was a serious guy, at least in his interviews. In person, he was a humble, friendly man who loved a good drink as much as we did. The hotel had a good-sized restaurant, a bar, and, as we found out later, a couples' swinger bar upstairs.

We had just driven in from somewhere in Maine and were dead tired. I believe we had just completed seventeen games straight without a day off and then had to drive to Long Island. We had a night off because of Monday Night Football. We had learned that we couldn't draw a crowd to watch our game on Monday nights since football had taken that slot. We went to the bar to have drinks and watch football.

When we first got to the bar, we all headed for tables with a view of the TV. A few went to the bar and sat on stools to watch. It was nearly halftime before anyone recognized Evel Knievel in the room; the bartender was keeping his presence low-key. Over in a corner of the bar next to a wall, Mr. Knievel and his bodyguard were sitting, having drinks and keeping to themselves. At halftime, one of our ladies asked the bartender if that man was Evel Knievel. The bartender nodded. She then told a couple of our group, and in a few minutes, we all knew he was there, but we understood that privacy was sacred, so no one approached him. We did, however, start sending drinks to his table from the Roller Derby crowd. Before long, he was engaging us in banter, and we were having fun kidding each other.

The football game wasn't interesting, and how often do you get to drink with the one and only Evel Knievel? We all had more than enough to drink, and since we were so tired, the booze hit us harder than usual. Several of us, including Mr. Knievel, decided to retire for the evening at about four o'clock in the morning. In New York, a club would stay open until the last patron had left.

The next night was game night for us, and we had invited Evel Knievel to join us. We didn't know he had performed on Sunday afternoon and had taken a bad fall, breaking or reinjuring one of his legs. Since he usually carried his silver cane, we didn't know he was injured. Apparently, he had fallen after jumping a thousand buses, or maybe it was a hundred buses. He'd slammed into the concrete wall at the coliseum. If he was in pain, he never let on. Of course, with all the booze we drank, none of us were feeling any pain.

CANADIAN BUS TRIPS

In 1973, Jerry Seltzer, the owner of the International Roller Derby League, sold his six skating teams to Bill Griffith's Roller Games. Jerry had had enough of the picketing from some of the players and the insinuations of prejudice against blacks. As a result of his selling the teams, Francine and I were shipped to Montreal, Francine's hometown. After a four-week engagement in Philadelphia, the Roller Games units traveled by team bus with both teams on the same bus. Since I skated and was in charge of transporting, erecting, and tearing down the track, I had a Dodge Maxi van for the track crew and myself. Francine rode on the bus with the teams and played poker and made more money than she did skating.

The team bus would usually load up early in the morning and drive to the next city. I would often leave after the track was torn down and placed into the semi, which meant Francine and I traveled apart for most of the next six months. My crew was made up of the new male skaters and the truck drivers. Just like in the Roller Derby, I negotiated a full eight hours of pay, five hours for setup and three hours for teardown. I allowed my crew to go as fast as we could in order to make bar time. I was all for that!

Canada, for the most part, had state and province liquor stores. That meant we had to buy our beer at the state stores and could not bring it into the dressing rooms on Sundays. However, Montreal was a French Canadian province, and beer was allowed seven days a week. Hard liquor was sold only in state stores, and bars had a beer bar and a separate bar for mixed drinks and hard liquor, such as brandy, scotch, and whiskey.

My crew, who usually had a few too many beers, would go to sleep while I drove us to the next city. On long trips, we consumed large quantities of beer and often had to restock in the closest city we could find. My crew were all great guys, and they all worked their butts off. Once, in Ontario, Norm Olsen, our Canadian promoter, watched how fast we tore down the track, and he decided we should only get one hour's pay instead of three. I told my guys to stop work, and they did, even though he threatened to fire them from track work and skating. We were on the road, and he did not have access to other skaters or a track crew. We waited till almost time for the fans to come into the building before setting up the track. The place was sold out. Norm blinked. We had won our protest. We set a record, setting up the track completely from the truck to the arena in only forty-six minutes. Norm never said a word about my crew again. He realized by watching them how hard they worked and how disciplined they were.

Over the years, there were several times when the truck arrived late because of bad weather or breakdowns. There were times when we had less than an hour before the game started, and the fans got a treat in watching the track setup. It was like a ballet.

THIRTY-FIVE DEGREES BELOW ZERO IN SUDBURY, ONTARIO

Can you believe it? In 1968, one of our games was scheduled in Sudbury, Ontario, Canada. We skated in Sudbury in a gorgeous arena with shouting crowds and screaming fans. We did so after driving the whole day before, when temperatures reached as low as 10 degrees with clear skies. The night of the game, many of the skaters left right after the game to get ahead of a cold spell that was coming in. That proved to be a smart thing to do.

Pete Boyd, Jo Jo Stafford, Don Drewry, and I stayed the night since we worked tearing down the track. Then we headed to the bar to have a couple of drinks. By the time we were ready to leave the bar, the temperature was already below zero and falling. By ten o'clock the next morning, we were heading to Montreal. We heard a weatherman say it was down to -35 degrees, and with the chill factor, it could be as low as -70.

We decided to take blankets from the hotel and wrap them around our legs to keep a little warmer. We tried to buy blankets from the clerk at the front desk, but he would not sell them at any price. He tried to convince us not to go out on the highway, which the Canadian Mounted Police had officially closed. Another tactic we used to stay warm was stuffing newspapers up our pant legs and inside our shirts. We realized the heater would not work, since the engine could not warm up enough to create the much-needed heat. Also, I wired cardboard to the car's grill in order to keep the engine from freezing while we drove.

For the first forty or fifty miles, I drove at about ten miles per hour, hugging the shoulder of the road to keep traction on the tires. Don Drewry was scraping the windshield from the inside in order to keep the ice off so that I could see to drive. The thermos of coffee we had in the front seat froze solid before we could enjoy the coffee. Pete Boyd and Jo Jo Stafford became good buddies in the backseat, holding each other in order to stay warm.

We made it out of the mountains and down to a warmer climate and found a café where we could wrap our cold hands around mugs of hot coffee and eat some warm food. We felt lucky to be alive. Driving in that weather was a stupid thing to do.

When we arrived in Montreal, the police were waiting for us. The hotel clerk had called ahead, hoping we would get arrested for stealing the blankets. After we explained the whole situation to the policemen, they let us pay a fine and took the blankets away from us. That night, after the game, we had several cold beers to celebrate our brush with death in the frozen north.

GUNS IN THUNDER BAY

In 1973, we were on a cross-country tour from Halifax, Nova Scotia, to Victoria Island, Vancouver, in British Columbia. One of our most memorable venues along the way was Thunder Bay, Ontario, known for its wild residents. You know the kind—drunk, boisterous, and willing to fight at the drop of a hat.

The game was a wild, thunderous event with fans throwing punches at each other in the stands and tossing beer bottles onto the track. The CMPs (Canadian Mounted Police) tried to keep order. During the game, I was knocked out, and the infield assistants and our box-office manager, Sal, a self-confessed former bagman for the Mafia, had to carry me off the track. Apparently, I came around just as Sal and some fans were mixing it up. Sal, a professional boxer until he lost an eye in a fight, said that I jumped off the stretcher and began attacking the guys who were assaulting him. That caused a few more of their friends to get involved. I don't know how many were engaged in the fight by the time the CMPs got things under control.

The fights were finally broken up, and the CMPs arrested a couple of people. But we won the game. Yeah! That night, we stayed in town at a hole-in-the-wall hotel right out of some Hollywood B movie. This was the only hotel that would take skaters as guests, because we had such a bad reputation. The hotel was one of those places where rooms were routinely rented by the hour. The door to our room would not lock, so I propped a chair against the door for some degree of security.

That night, we heard fights in the halls, gunshots, and yelling. We tried calling the police, but the switchboard would not respond. We stayed huddled in our bed, praying for the break of dawn to arrive so that we could leave this godforsaken part of Canada. When morning finally arrived, Francine and I walked down the hall through beer and wine bottles, cigarette butts, and vomit. It was not a pretty sight. We discovered that most of the skaters had opted to drive all night to our next stop instead of staying at that hotel. Francine never let me forget how I placed her in danger in that hotel from hell.

HARRY MORGAN, NATIONAL FLAT-TRACK SPEED CHAMPION OF 1970, AND THE HUNDRED-LAP MATCH RACE AT THE PHILADELPHIA SPECTRUM ARENA, FEBRUARY 1973

Harry Morgan was a fast and tough skater. Size-wise, he and I were about the same height, weight, and build. I could stay with him on the track at all speeds. Flat-track skaters always had a hard time using centrifugal force to work for them, and they often entered the turns a couple of feet off the mark. They would try to power out of the turn too late, so they lost the speed they built up in the straightaway in the turns. Since Harry and I seemed to be jamming against each other, it was only a matter of time before he and I would end up fighting. During one TV night, we got into a fight that stretched throughout the entire game. The night ended with me beating the crap out of Harry, and during a postgame TV interview, Harry came up with the idea of challenging me to a hundred-lap speed race. Such a challenge had never been done in the Roller Derby. Most challenge races were only five to six laps, not one hundred.

The fans started calling the TV station, wanting to know when the challenge would take place. Keep in mind that Harry and I were jammers, which meant we often skated fifteen to twenty miles a game. In addition to that, we would have to skate at top speed for a five-mile race. Thank God the producers and coaches realized we would need to train for several weeks during the regular season to be able to add this speed-and-endurance race to our schedule. In light of all the calls from fans during the first week of the challenge, it was decided the race would be held at the Philly Spectrum, which, at that time, could seat about twelve thousand people.

Over the next month, Harry and I trained together five days a week. We were constantly pushing each other to go faster and longer. After the first week, I suggested to Harry that we use wooden wheels like those skaters had used at the start of the Roller Derby back in the 1930s. One problem with wooden wheels was that they could easily lose traction on the Masonite track we used. Also, wooden wheels often overheated and came loose, causing the skater to possibly lose a wheel or two.

After some trial and error, we found that if we put Elmer's glue on the ends of the axles, the wheels wouldn't fall off. Additionally, we learned that if the track was sprinkled with plaster of paris just before the race started, we could maintain speed and the groove of the track. This would help us keep our speed up, since the wooden wheels were only about one-third the weight of the polyurethane wheels. Interestingly, we didn't fight or argue during the training, but every night, we would have a knock-down, drag-out fight in the games.

Two days before our race, Harry came down with mononucleosis, a common disease of the '70s. The disease robs you of your strength, and all you want to do is sleep. The Spectrum was already sold out, and the promoters refused to cancel and reschedule, as our team would be heading for Montreal the next day for a three-month Canadian tour. It was decided that James Trotter, the men's captain of the Philly team, would do the race. The race would be held at halftime. James was not an endurance skater, nor was he known for his speed. Additionally, it was a big mistake for James to skate using wooden wheels without any practice sessions. I did my best to talk him out of it and even replaced my wooden wheels with the polyurethane ones to make the race fairer.

For some reason, the promoters had advertised and promoted this race as "Old Man" Larry Smith against the young national flat-track speed champion. I was twenty-nine at the time, and Harry was twenty-six. Go figure.

The first half of the game was brutal. Jim got his butt kicked pretty well, and my teammates did a good job of softening him up. However, I was out on almost every jam. The other team took revenge on our jammers, leaving me to score as much as possible to keep the game close. In the dressing room, I could see that Jim was fatigued and concerned. I tried once again, without success, to get him to keep his normal wheels and not use the wooden ones.

When the time came for us to start the race, Jim fell down twice getting to the track and fell again when he tried to stand up on the track. I hammed it up by going into the infield and doing pushups and jumping jacks or just skating around to give Jim a bad time. Finally, we lined up on the track, and the referee blew his starting whistle. The race was on! I was already a half lap ahead of Jim after the first lap. I decided to give the fans their money's worth by playing up the old-man gambit. Every time I pulled a couple of laps ahead, I stopped and dropped down to do a few pushups while Jim caught up.

The fans ate this up. They were going crazy, watching me play the rabbit and Jim play the tortoise. About fifty laps into the race, Jim lost two of his wheels and took a bad fall. While the skate boy changed his wheels back to polyurethane ones, I did pushups and jumping jacks, danced a little, and taunted the crowd while Jim rested. By the time we restarted the race, Jim had caught his breath, and now, with his regular wheels, he had his speed and confidence back. At that point, I was exhausted from all my exercise and clowning around.

Unbeknownst to me, the referee switched from a whistle to a starter's pistol. When he shot the gun, I fell down and covered my head with my hands, partly from the shock of the gun and partly to be a ham. The fans were hysterical. Jim was almost a lap ahead of me, and I was tired. By the time we came to the final three laps, Jim and I were neck and neck and started blocking each other, even though that was not part of the rules for this race. Jim knocked me down, so I got back up and knocked him down. As we headed for the finish line, I started running on my skates. I tripped and fell just as Jim went over the finish line ahead of me. It was a real "The Tortoise and the Hare" race after all.

That night, at the end of the game, they brought in our prize money for the race. You see, in the Roller Derby, a match race paid big money, sometimes more than a week's salary for each participant, no matter who won the race. Jim worked for the Roller Games League and received a check for twenty-five dollars. I worked for the International Roller Derby League, which earned me 1 percent of the gate receipts: more than $1,800. You should have seen the look on Jim's face; it was priceless. Harry Morgan even asked Jim to split the twenty-five dollars since he'd had to do all the training. I can't repeat Jim's reply.

That was the last time I got to skate against Harry or Jim and the last time they billed me as the old man.

HOCKEY ARENAS: PLYWOOD VERSUS ICE

When I joined the Roller Derby, it was common for a track crew consisting of ten men to take six hours to set up and another four hours to tear down and pack the track up into the truck for transport to our next destination. Because of the large amount of time this took, the number of venues the Roller Derby could book was limited, especially at hockey arenas during their season. Also, many high-school gyms were too small for our standard track, which was 50 feet wide by 120 feet long. In the early '60s, Gil Orozco of the Bombers and his track crew, which I was a part of, started to develop a method that would cut down the amount of time it took to assemble the track, making the skating track more flexible for different venues.

Imagine, if you will, that by 1973, our record for setting up a track, with only an eight-member track crew made up of male and female skaters, was forty-five minutes for complete setup and thirty-five minutes to tear down and pack up. We accomplished this on Victoria Island, British Columbia, Canada, as the crew was working to catch the ferry back into Vancouver. Leading up to this, we found during the off-season while building new tracks that we could set the track up as each piece came out of the truck.

We learned this by watching stagehands set up scenery for shows. We came up with the idea to build a ramp and use stage carts to carry the pieces of track off and into the truck. We were able to reduce the amount of crew needed for the job by two people. We bargained for a guarantee of five hours' pay to set up and three hours' pay to tear down, no matter how long the job actually took. That gave our crew strong incentive to do the job faster. Since skaters were doing the work, they made sure no corners were cut and ensured skater safety.

We changed the track layout to incorporate nuts and lock washers to keep the uprights from coming apart, as well as intermediate braces to add strength. We used a large dolly with four-feet-high sides to keep the upright pieces from falling apart when we moved them. As the truck was being unloaded, the person inside the truck would help load the stage cart with a piece of track. The person manning the cart then transported the piece of track inside while the rest of the crew waited to attach the uprights and track pieces together. The two carts were moving all the time until the truck was empty. The setup crew attached the pieces and the uprights while someone underneath the track installed the intermediate braces and secured a center bolt halfway down the track piece.

While all of this was happening, another person laid twenty-four-inch Masonite pieces between two track sections, forming a smooth joint for the skating surface. At the same time, the female skaters working on the track began installing padding on the uprights and the outside rails, as well as on the kickboards encircling the track. I usually worked the inside of the truck, and by the time it was empty, the crew inside would be laying the last piece of track, performing what we called "the marriage" by joining the two final track pieces. I busied myself by helping to secure the Masonite surface, attaching braces, or doing whatever was left to do.

Setup was an awesome sight to watch, and many building managers and workers would come out to watch the track ballet. When we skated in hockey arenas, their games finished about an hour before our game was supposed to start, and there we were, almost ready to skate. On the hockey ice, we had the arena staff lay sheets of plywood over the ice to give a stable skating surface to the infield. With ice underneath, the boards often became wet, cold, and slick. Coming off the track going thirty miles per hour and hitting the icy plywood was a scary situation, but it was not as bad as hitting solid ice at thirty miles per hour. If you went over the rails after being hit, you landed on hard ice. It was tricky to get back up on your skates and back onto the track.

Along with hockey arenas, we could now skate at high-school fund-raisers. All we had to do was take several straightaway pieces out of our track, and we had a fifty-by-ninety-foot track, which was a better configuration for us to skate on. We could do what was called a five-stride, a normal stride that produced a lot of speed, on each half of the track. When we used the extra straightaway pieces, we had to do an awkward seven-stride. Many high schools learned that the Roller Derby was a successful fund-raiser, which caused us to be in constant demand for live performances.

A couple of times, they put us in buildings so small that we had to remove four straightaway pieces, making the track almost a circle rather than an oval. Bad idea! Everyone was getting dizzy, and when that happened, people were often injured. Fortunately, we only had a couple of games like that, and the injuries were minor broken bones and cuts that required stitches.

Over the years, I looked back on my track-building experience as fondly as I do my skating career. We were engineering on the fly using trial and error along with loads of innovation. Gil Orozco, Bill Morrissey, Dave Cannella, James Pierce, and I made a lot of changes that really paid off for the track crews, the arenas, and fans who otherwise might have missed an opportunity to watch a live Roller Derby game.

MONTREAL TRAINING SCHOOL

In April of 1967, I was sent home with a major nose fracture and a deviated septum. I was advised it would take me four to five weeks to recuperate before I could return to active skating. That was all well and good, but how would I pay my bills on disability insurance? I called Jerry Seltzer to see if he had any work I could do at the administrative office. He told me to come to his office in Oakland, California, to discuss an opportunity that had just opened up. Needless to say, I was glad for the possibility of some kind of available work. After arriving in Oakland, I was escorted into Jerry's private office in the Kaiser Building. I took a seat that allowed me to enjoy the magnificent view from his corner office window. He offered me coffee or soda, and after some small talk, he asked if I would consider going to Montreal to open a training facility for the new Fleur De Lys Canadian team that he and Norman Olsen of Montreal were putting together. Jerry had heard about the training school I had run in Phoenix while I was skating semipro and how I'd conducted some classes at the Oakland training center.

Well, the idea of going to Montreal alone was a little daunting since I didn't speak French. I had only skated there a couple of times and would be starting from scratch, which caused me some concern. Jerry went on to explain that his dad, Leo Seltzer, who was one of the creators of the sport, and his mother would be there in the beginning. I said yes even though my legs were shaking and my heart was racing. I knew I could do it. After all, life is about taking risks and chasing your dreams. How bad could it be?

A few days later, I was on an Air Canada flight out of San Francisco with a small suitcase, a notebook, and an English-to-French translation book. After arrival, I caught a taxi to the Hotel Sherbrook, where my team had stayed a few months earlier. The next morning, I contacted Mr. Olsen's office and made an appointment to talk about all the details. I needed to know if a suitable building was available for the school. Did we have the proper permits? Did he know people I could hire to help move the track inside after it arrived, as well as a couple of assistants to help with the daily duties?

Mr. O. only knew that we had a building and said his man Sal would show me around the place. Sal and I drove over to the building, which was located in the Rosemont District, a predominately French-speaking area. The building had a bar and little cigarette shop downstairs, in addition to remnants of a bowling alley upstairs, complete with grooves in the cement floor where the bowling lanes had been, as well as metal straps and holes in the floor. The building had an elevator, stairs, and a formal entry that would work as a staging area for the office, skate booth, and rest area. There were lots of windows, which provided plenty of light, and the ceiling was high enough to accommodate the track and skaters. The major problems were the second-floor location and the small elevator that would be used to bring the track sections in. Unknown to me, Leo Seltzer had already called a news conference, even though the track had not arrived from the States. I arranged with Sal to have an eight-man crew waiting to help unload the track, set it up, and get it ready for the news conference Leo had scheduled. The track arrived a day and a half late. I led our inexperienced French-speaking crew at a breakneck pace in the task of getting the track in the building one piece at a time. I was securing the Masonite to the track as the print news and TV crews were busy talking with Leo and Norman. The media wanted pictures of someone skating, so I laced up my skates, washed the sweat from my brow, and took to the track like a circus monkey. I skated around at full speed, took a few falls, and flipped over the rails to the delight of the film crews. This was our prepresentation to the Montreal public.

We advertised all week for our grand-opening night, and the media ran our story complete with former Bay Bomber Larry Smith in his jeans and sweatshirt, skating, falling, and flipping to the delight of the well-fed and boozed-up media in attendance. Just days before the opening, I built an office and a skate storage room and smoothed out the infield area of the track as best I could. I hired two local guys, cousins Raymond Anderson and Tico St. Jacque, to help with the daily work. The day of our grand opening, Tico, Raymond, and I were busy washing, cleaning, painting, and generally sprucing the place up. Leo and Norman had me scheduled on two newscasts the evening before we opened to maximize the hype. Before going downtown to the TV stations, I asked Raymond and Tico to wash the floors one final time. I was unaware that my enterprising helpers decided to use the fire hose to wash down the track, infield, and reception area. It was not a bad idea if one knew how to control the water flow from a fire hose. Remember this space used to be a bowling alley, and the spots where the lanes had been bolted down now had holes in the floor that went all the way through. The bar down below had covered its ceiling with acoustic ceiling tiles in order to hide the holes.

My brain trust, Raymond and Tico, were on the news that night as well, arguing with the owner of the bar, who had a gun. That's right— the bar owner came upstairs with his gun and held my two geniuses at gunpoint while the police tried to persuade him to let them go with the assurance that Leo and the Roller Derby would pay for the damage to his bar. When I returned to the school, it was packed with police, reporters, and our new trainees waiting for their shot at stardom. It was a total madhouse.

Finally, Raymond and Tico were released to help pass out the new skates. Leo went to the track to begin basic training, while I was responsible for coordinating the mini–box office and skate concession. As I began putting the new skaters though their initial turns around the track, some of them began to bring me skates that already needed repair. I found that the ball bearings had disintegrated. In the rush to start training, Leo had ordered the skates from the number-one ice-hockey skate company in all of Canada. He'd purchased these skates from a European skate vendor who'd supplied us with basic dance skates that had defective bearings and ten-degree trucks.

I spent the first two weeks fixing skates until our new Roller Derby–style Chicago-built forty-five-degree-angle trucks with high-speed bearings arrived. After a few days, we had everyone equipped with the new skates. By this time, Leo had four groups of intermediate skaters ready for me to train. He would take the beginners for an hour and a half, and then I would take over with the intermediate skaters. We had two groups of women and two groups of men. The average group contained twelve skaters. I would take the women through pacing and wind sprints, and as they rested, I took the men through the same procedures. I taught them how to fall, take a rail without breaking a rib, and stop. Later, I taught them blocking, elbow smashes, hip blocks, and jump blocks.

Many of these kids had grown up on ice skates, and they were in good physical condition. However, skating on the banked wooden track with speed skates was a lot different from skating on ice. As you might expect, they wanted to try everything they had seen on TV, including beating each other up. In a few weeks, I divided them into four teams, and we started having actual games on weekends. During the week, I moved a couple of the girls onto the men's training teams; including Francine Cochu, winner of the Rookie of the Year award in 1967, who later became my wife.

By August, we had developed a full team of professional Roller Derby skaters, the Fleur De Lys, and we took them to Philadelphia to skate two games against the Philly team. We got our butts kicked, but we only lost the first game by two points and the second game by one point. After returning, we took the two teams, the new Canadian All Stars and the Fleur De Lys, on a six-week road trip across central Canada. When we returned to Montreal, I was sent home to rejoin the Bay Bombers, and in a few weeks, the Fleur De Lys came to the San Francisco Bay Area for a two-week engagement.

The training experience in Montreal is one of my most memorable times. I met Francine and taught lots of young people how to be Roller Derby skaters. Their dreams and mine were realized. There were many who tried out and didn't make the cut. We had Norman Ardweny, a one-eyed, hard-skating young man who worked harder than anyone else who made the team but broke a leg in his first game. He never got another opportunity to be a Roller Derby pro. Then there was a young mother of almost thirty years of age who came down from a small farm town outside Quebec City to give skating a try. She was good enough but couldn't travel because of her parental responsibilities. There was a newspaper printer who helped in many ways. He was over thirty years old and couldn't give up his job at the newspaper to travel, but he had the talent and the heart. I will always remember that little training school, the people, the circumstances, and my love for Montreal.

BILLIE JEAN KING AND FRANCINE COCHU

I'm sure many of you remember when Billie Jean King beat Bobbie Fisher in a nationally televised tennis match. The match was highly publicized, and the Roller Derby game that had been originally scheduled was changed so that we wouldn't compete with the televised event. The Roller Derby had learned that it could not compete with TV sports. The lines were drawn between male and female as to who could win the match. After all, males were considered stronger, faster, and more adept in sports than females. The prevailing understanding—or should I say misunderstanding—was that men ruled.

Those who are familiar with that era know what happened: Billie Jean kicked Bobby's butt. This made Billie Jean King famous and a household name. Women now could compete equally with men. Fans of the Roller Derby knew that the female skaters competed under the same rules and that it was the combined score that counted in a Roller Derby game. Men and women, while they did not skate against each other, played by the same rules. The points were combined at the end of the game, with the winners being the team with the highest total.

With the nation hungry for equality, Billie Jean King was a hot ticket on talk shows, along with Joanie Weston of the Bay Bombers, and in Canada, my wife, Francine Cochu, got lots of invitations to appear on national and local talk shows with Billie Jean King. I had the pleasure of being the unseen husband following Francine and Miss King on the talk-show circuit. After the show, we would head to a club for drinks.

Just think about the impact the Roller Derby had on professional women's sports, not to mention the quest for equal rights. This occurred at about the time when Gloria Steinem started writing about the insanity of women not having equal rights. It seems ironic to me that Miss King and Francine never talked about this issue outside of the interview platform. They were content with small talk about fashion, tennis, and the Roller Derby.

NIGERIAN ANTOINE GILMORE

In 1970, Antoine Gilmore emigrated from Nigeria and joined the Roller Derby. His English-language skills were good, and he was a pleasant young man. He was about five feet three and maybe 150 pounds. That was an excellent size for a jammer. He worked hard and was a team player as well as a good poker player. He was also quite the ladies' man. In fact, that was his real claim to fame in the Roller Derby. You see, Antoine had the ability to attract Holiday Inn maids. If your room was to be cleaned by the same maid who cleaned Antoine's room, you often had to wait for your room to be finished, because Antoine was busy entertaining the maid.

The problem became evident when we skated in South Bend, Indiana. Francine and I had skated for five months with the Chicago Pioneers, and we were now based in South Bend. Typically, we stayed at the Holliday Inn when we were in town. Antoine was entertaining several maids there, which caused a lot of conflict. We were always waiting for our room to be cleaned. We finally asked our road manager to get involved, in addition to the hotel manager. Before all was said and done, four maids were fired, and Antoine was sent home. He lost his Roller Derby dream because of passion and lust. It's a good lesson for us all.

PARLEZ-VOUS FRANÇAIS?

Learning to speak English after living in French Montreal all one's life, not to mention only attending French-speaking schools, might have been a handicap for some, but not for Francine. She learned her new language by the most favorable method: she lived and worked with people who only spoke English. Additionally, her husband only knew a few phrases of French and deliberately only spoke English so that she would have to learn it.

When Francine and I first started dating, we went on double dates with couples who were bilingual. We always had someone to interpret for us. That lasted for about four weeks before we found ourselves on our own. Two months after we started dating, I was sent home to San Francisco to join the Bay Bombers. Francine and her Canadian team would join us for a series a few weeks later. While with the Bombers, I managed to take a rail, breaking my ankle. I was out of commission for a few weeks. While mending, I often sat by the pool with my English-to-French conversion book and my writing pad, working on love letters to Francine. She and her mom had a big laugh about my scribbling.

Later, when Francine joined me in the Bay Area, we were together for two weeks before she left for Montreal once again. I worked on my French and called her almost every night, and I wrote her a letter a day, even though she could barely understand them. She did, however, understand that I had fallen in love with her.

The next time we met up, we were on our way to Chicago. She was skating on the Pioneers, while I was on the Bay Bombers. We were touring on what was intended to be a six-month trip, but it ended early because of low attendance at the games. Normally, we would be on the road from January through the middle of May and then skate in the San Francisco Bay Area from May until mid-October. We would generally be off from mid-October until January. That year, we tried to skate from November straight through May. When the closure was announced, I asked her to marry me. She said yes.

I was amazed at Francine's tenacity for learning English. The girls were always telling Francine and Judy Sinnet, a bilingual Canadian skater who made the tour with Francine, to speak English. I was told that Joan Weston and Annie Calvello were the most vocal in the girls' dressing room. Also, Francine loved American soap operas and learned a lot of English by watching the shows every day. Additionally, by traveling all over the United States—given all the various dialects, from the southern drawl to the loud and snappy New York way of speaking to the Maine and New Hampshire twangs—she developed an accent that had people asking where she was from.

Today she works for a Mercedes-Benz dealer in Pleasanton, California. She is an administrator and receptionist backup. Only a slight accent is left in her speech, and it is charming.

SAL THE BAGMAN

One of the most colorful people I worked with in the Roller Derby was Sal, a former bagman for the Canadian Mafia, as well as a prizefighter. Now, this guy was a legitimate low-level Mafia guy. He was also our box-office manager in the Canadian skating group.

My first meeting with Sal happened when I went to Montreal to open up the Roller Derby training center. I was told to meet a guy at a Jewish deli on Sherbrook Street who would help me get what I needed. I arrived early to find a guy who looked like a Mafia guy, or at least a gangster of some sort. I could have sworn I had seen him in the movies, portraying a villain. Sal recognized me from my Roller Derby photos. He stood about six feet two and weighed 220 pounds. He was in his early forties and sported blue khaki-style pants with a polo shirt accented by a winter jacket. He smiled and shook my hand with his big, oversized mitts. He yelled something in Jewish or French to the guys behind the counter and then asked me if I wanted something to drink. I requested a beer, and he replied that the beer would go well with the pastrami and Swiss on dark rye that he had ordered for me. Sal was a take-charge kind of guy.

We sat at a little table while he removed his glass eye and then washed it in the glass of water the waiter had placed on the table. Then, using his spoon as a mirror, he placed his glass eye back into his eye socket. He did this while firing questions at me without taking a breath. I could see this was going to be fun. Sal was all business. He wanted to know what I needed and all the details: How many men did I need?

What tools would I need? How long would it take to get the track into Montreal from the States? How soon did I want to look at the building they had selected? Had I found a place to live? How long had I been doing this? What did I think of Montreal? This is just a sample of the many questions he asked.

Before he finished asking his questions, we were served our sandwiches and beers. Sal dove right in and started eating. I caught my breath and starting eating as well. This was my first experience eating pastrami and Swiss on dark rye. Wow, this was a hit! As I began to answer Sal's questions, he relaxed and smiled in a way that let me know we were going to be friends. He talked about his days as a prizefighter and told me how he'd lost his eye during a fight. He recounted his days as a bagman for the local Mafia, which I thought was bull, and how he had attempted to do a hit but the gun had jammed. After that, he'd decided not to become a made guy, which is the Mafia term for someone who completes a hit for the Mafia.

Over the next few weeks, Sal and I spent almost every day having breakfast or lunch while discussing the progress of the school. Once the school opened, I hardly saw him. He returned to do work for Mr. O., the local promoter and former wrestler. When Leo Seltzer put the training center in my hands, Sal and I had lunch, and he told me some of his stories, although he knew I didn't believe him. After several months, Sal said he wanted to take me to visit his friends and play some cards. He said I would just have to watch and listen while not commenting on what I heard being discussed. Additionally, by no means could I repeat what I heard to anyone outside the card room.

Sal drove us through a downtown area of Montreal to a rather seedy-looking restaurant with the proverbial back room, where, sitting around four card tables, guys who looked more like gangsters than Sal were laughing, smoking, and playing cards. When I walked in, they all stopped talking and looked at Sal and me. Sal immediately introduced me as the world's greatest skater and said, "Don't worry; he can be trusted. He's with me." So they told me to take a seat and offered me a beer. Sal sat down and started playing cards. They played a form of gin rummy and were betting in cash. When a player got up to leave, he would settle up, shake my hand, and tell me to come back someday.

The game went on for about three hours, and during this time, Sal ordered lunch for us and some more beer for me. As I sat there listening, I heard discussion about some things I had seen on TV, including truck heists and such. It made me more than a little nervous. More than once, someone spoke to Sal in French, and they would look my way. Sal tried to ease the tension by repeating in French the words for "my friend."

Later on, we took two teams from the training school on the road, and Sal was managing the box office and all the cash. Sal was always on time and ready to lend a helping hand. He especially took care of Francine, as if he were her bodyguard. He took her shopping at the local stores, and after they returned, he always had small gifts for her. Francine became alarmed that he was flirting with her. When I asked him about it, he convinced me she was more like his daughter and was just a friend. After the three of us talked, we all relaxed and understood that this was just Sal's way of being a friend.

My friend Sal had a problem: he was a kleptomaniac. He would steal something every day, and he was giving stolen items to Francine. She once witnessed him going into a men's store, trying on a jacket, and then walking outside with it. The store owner ran after him, asking what he thought he was doing. Sal said, "I just wanted to see how it would look in the sunlight." He then took off the jacket and told the shop owner he could keep it. Later that day, he went back and got the jacket; we don't know if he paid for it or not.

Later, when Francine and I were married and had returned to the Roller Games Canadian All Stars after the closing of the real Roller Derby, Sal was once again our bagman—or should I say our box-office manager. Sal discovered we had several thousand old Roller Derby newspapers from when the Roller Derby had been in town, and he asked me to have them stored in the front storage area of the truck carrying our track. He wanted to sell them at the arenas for a dollar each. I told him he was crazy. He sold them and gave me half of the proceeds for helping him with the project. The guy was always thinking. Once, when we traveled to Toronto during a Roller Derby tour, he introduced me to world-famous Canadian wrestler Andre the Giant. Andre was seven feet three and weighed about four hundred pounds, but he was not fat. He was a giant. Another time, Sal introduced me to Bobby, a friend of his who had just gotten back from the States after doing a job. Bobby was a real hit man.

On another occasion, while we were skating in Thunder Bay, Ontario, Sal tried to help a skater who was being attacked by fans. I jumped off the stretcher they were taking me out on and joined in. We had a great fight with the unruly fans. From that point on, Sal and I had a strong bond of friendship. I knew I could always count on him, and he could count on me as well. I haven't heard from Sal since 1975 and fear he has long since passed away. The telephone number I had for him was disconnected, and my mail to him was returned as undeliverable.

PAUL "THE BEAR" RUPERT

In 1973, Francine and I were on the Ohio Jolters, which had been sold to the National Skating Derby, and the Canadian All Stars. We toured the eastern states until March and then went to Canada, where our home base was in Montreal, Quebec. This was Francine's dream—she was finally living and skating in her hometown. We took day trips into the surrounding communities and occasionally bus trips to other provinces. Then, in May, we started a road trip to Halifax, Nova Scotia, followed by a trip to Victoria Island, British Columbia, before returning home to Montreal.

Our men's captain was Paul "the Bear" Rupert, while our women's captain was Jan Vallow. I spent most of my time as a jammer as well as the construction foreman responsible for setting up and tearing down the track—a job I loved more than performing. I say "performing" because the National Skating Derby was a show. We were not a fast-paced sport any longer. We were told when and how to score or when to get knocked down or beaten up. The charade was a bit embarrassing for us. Francine and I made it to Victoria Island and then returned as far as Winnipeg before we quit.

Paul was a natural for the role of good-guy Canadian woodsman. The hometown fans loved him. Every night, Paul would get the crap beaten out of him, or at least it looked as if he did. Then he would come to the rescue of little Frankie Macedo, turn the tables on the bad guys, and beat the crap out of them. For all his antics, Paul was a good skater and pretty fast for his size. He always treated me fairly, understanding that I was done with the show and only going through the motions. I know he would have fired me if it weren't for Francine. She was born in Montreal and was the Canadian sweetheart. She did her best to give a great performance in light of all the clowning around going on around her. She was a real pro.

When we arrived in Vancouver, British Columbia, Francine and I called our home to talk with Mr. and Mrs. Charles Filloon, who were house-sitting for us. They had received an official-looking registered letter for us, so I asked them to open it. The letter contained our cash-out on the profit-sharing program that Jerry Seltzer had set up for us a few years before he sold out to the National Skating Derby. The check was more than a full year's salary for Francine and me. This meant we could quit and start our lives over. We flew home right after the Victoria Island game, and in a couple of days, Mr. O., the Canadian promoter, called and offered us double and then triple our weekly salary if we would return to the road trip.

Francine was already having second thoughts about our decision to quit, so we agreed.

When we returned, the animosity of the other skaters was clear. By the time we reached Winnipeg, Francine had had enough. During the second girls' period, she was skating with all her heart, when some of the other team members started an obviously fake fight. The crowd was booing, and some even started to leave the arena, shouting, "Fake! Fake!" Francine was devastated and skated into the infield, crying. When I went to her, she told me through her tears that she wanted to go home. She'd had enough. We skated off the track and into our separate dressing rooms to shower and change into street clothes. I met her in the hallway leading to the parking lot and asked her again if she was sure about the decision to quit. She said she just couldn't do it anymore. We had fought the image of a fake sport for our entire careers, and now there we were, doing what we had said we would never do. Don't get me wrong—Roller Games had many great skaters; however, the promoters forced everyone to skate a different style of game.

Back at our hotel, I ordered a bottle of our favorite wine. We held each other and enjoyed our wine before getting a good night's sleep. The next morning, I called the airport and was able to book a flight that was leaving in just a few hours. We got back to our home in San Leandro, leaving behind Rupert and the Roller Games to start the next chapter of our lives.

SUICIDE IN TORONTO

A memory that will haunt me to my grave is the suicide of a young eighteen-year-old Canadian boy outside of Toronto at the end of a horrific week. The week began, as most weeks in Canada did, with us hopscotching over the provinces of Canada. Our schedule made little sense, with us doubling back and forth from town to town. Mr. O., our local promoter, who was a former wrestler and now the co-owner of the Canadian All Stars, had Francine and me traveling ahead of the teams to do radio, newspaper, and TV spots. I was running the track crew as well, which I learned was too many jobs for one person.

We stayed in New London, Ontario, after a Friday-night game in some no-name town. We were scheduled to skate there on Saturday, with a Sunday-afternoon game in Toronto following a hockey game. We were to make the 175-mile drive to Toronto, skate, and then drive back. That meant I had to leave early with the track crew in order to set up immediately after the hockey game. We had our game and then tore down the track and drove back to New London.

The hockey game was a sell-out, and the crowd was slowly leaving the building. My crew did a great job of setting up, finishing in just one hour and ten minutes—a new record for us. Our game went well, and we had a sell-out as well. The fans loved us, and we won. After the game, my crew and I took the track down and had a couple of beers in the dressing room before heading back.

Our truck driver, Super Clutch, was from Montreal. He wasn't the best driver we ever had, but our backup driver was still in the learning process. Super Clutch told everyone that while he was in the military, he was part of a Special Forces unit. He had a big tattoo on his arm of the Special Forces insignia. Soon after, one of our skaters challenged him—and found out in short order that Super Clutch was a fraud. He couldn't fight his way out of a wet paper bag. Furthermore, he was afraid to fight, which only made things worse. Everyone gave him a bad time, I believe more for the lying than anything else. He was okay as a driver and didn't deserve what happened on the way back to New London.

Highway 401 was a good four-lane road separated by a broad ditch. It was pretty flat, with only a few turns. The truck left a few minutes ahead of the track crew. The road was so flat that we could see a good five to ten miles ahead of us. We saw billowing black smoke on the horizon. All of us thought there was a car on fire, and we were right. However, as we got closer, we realized it was our tractor trailer that was on fire. The cab was on fire, and the wind was blowing the flames away from the trailer carrying our track and uniforms. By the time we got closer to the truck, most of traffic had pulled to the side of the highway. They were not going to pass the flaming truck, out of fear that the diesel tanks might explode at any moment.

I went sliding up behind the trailer and stopped at an awkward angle. I could see the rear of the tractor, and under the trailer, I could see what appeared to be a car sandwiched under the frame and fifth wheel housing. At that moment, a thought hit me: the occupant or occupants must be dead. No one could have survived the crash. Super Clutch and two of our crew who had caught a ride with him were standing near the flaming truck. Super Clutch was as white as a bedsheet, jabbering about how it wasn't his fault. The other two skaters backed up his story, as if they were afraid he would be blamed for the accident.

I ran to the back of the trailer, opened the rear door, and climbed inside to see if our track was in jeopardy. I climbed all the way to the back and could feel the heat from the burning tractor, but so far, the track and uniforms were safe. I yelled at the guys to form a chain so that we could remove as much from the trailer as possible before it caught fire. After a few minutes, the Royal Canadian Police arrived, followed closely by a fire truck. They made me get out of the now-flaming trailer, and the firemen quickly put out the flames. The police were upset with me for caring so much about the contents of the truck. I tried to explain that we would have to shut down and would be out of business for a couple of weeks if we lost the track and uniforms. Fortunately, there was a spare track in California, though it needed some repair before it could be shipped to us.

The police impounded the trailer and what was left of the tractor because they had been involved in a fatal accident, which we later found out was a suicide. Apparently, the young man had just broken up with his girlfriend and was drinking and driving. Some of his friends were chasing him in their cars, trying to get him to pull over, but when they got close to him, he aimed straight for the truck and hit it head-on. Because of the height of the wheels and cab on the tractor trailer, the young man's car was smashed under the tractor's front end and rear wheels. The car burst into flames, causing the truck to ignite as well. We were lucky that Super Clutch and the crew members got out without any serious injuries.

We missed a couple of bookings before the authorities released the contents of the trailer to us. We transferred the contents to another trailer and headed to Montreal. Unloading the track was eerie. I could almost feel the young man's presence in the trailer as I slid the pieces of track out to the waiting carts.

The police cleared Super Clutch, but he quit the Roller Derby. We had another driver flown in temporarily until our backup driver passed the Canadian truck driver's license test. The thought of that young man's despair and his parents' anguish continues to haunt me. I only pray he is in God's hands today.

TALK STORY

The Hawaiian people have a custom called a "talk story." Talk stories are a means of telling stories of people and things that have passed and a way of saving the spirits and history of those people and things we want to preserve. Before written history, many people used this method to pass the verbal history of customs, ancestry, and folklore down to the next generation. So why should we be different?

A talk story comes to mind of Bill Morrissey in his 1970 Ford station wagon and the terrible automobile accident he and his passengers survived. We'd had another string of fifteen games in a row without a day off, and ahead of us was a thousand-mile trip somewhere. During a heavy snowstorm, Bill left in his car with three other skaters after packing up the track. As the story goes, Bill had driven for a couple of hours and was looking for a gas station, when he suddenly hit a snowdrift on the highway, which put his car into a spin that ultimately ended with the car landing in the divider between the highway lanes. The car rolled over a couple of times, throwing Bill and his passengers around. They were not wearing seat belts, and one of the passengers suffered a broken leg. Bill and the others had only bruises, small cuts, and a story to tell.

I know God was watching over all of us on the road, and considering the number of miles driven, the condition of the roads, and the driver's fatigue, we were lucky no one was killed or seriously injured in car accidents. I know a broken leg is serious, but it is not life threatening.

Bill rented a car to continue the road trip and bought a new car when we got back to the San Francisco Bay Area.

Bomb Threats

During the late 1960s, there was a lot of social unrest and civil disobedience surrounding the Vietnam War, resulting in a fad of people calling in bomb threats to cause government buildings to be emptied, thereby disrupting the daily flow of business. Threats then started coming in at sporting events, schools, and hotels. We had our own version of a bomb-threat caller. I won't identify him, since I promised to carry his secret to my grave. After several weeks of games without a day off, one of our own called in a bomb threat, causing the game to be canceled. A couple of weeks later, he did it again in Michigan. This time, the skaters took a vote to go ahead with the game, and most of the fans stayed. The FBI started an investigation that made our friendly caller nervous. I'm glad he stopped before they caught him, since that was a serious federal offense.

Valentine Butt

That's right—that's what we called her behind her back. The poor girl had a rather large, heart-shaped derriere that looked like a valentine. She was a pack skater and filled out a jersey well, and she liked to travel—two traits rookies needed. Unfortunately, she was a terrible driver, and only by the grace of God did her passengers survive. She loved to pass cars on two-lane roads even when it was not safe to do so. One problem she had as a skater was that she couldn't jump. I took it upon myself to teach her how after she had a couple of crashes into other skaters, when she could have jumped to avoid them. I put a Kleenex box on the track and had her skate around and then jump the box. She couldn't do it in the first several attempts, but after some coaching, she was ready to move up to a trash can laid on its side and then to a folded chair laid flat on the track, and by the time we ended our session, she was doing multiple jumps over cardboard boxes. I thought we had succeeded with the training, but in the next game, the pack did a subway, a move in which the whole pack falls down, and V-Butt skated right into the backs of the other skaters instead of jumping over them. It wasn't long afterward that she was replaced by another rookie. That's how it goes on the road.

Poker Games

A tradition that started at the beginning of the Roller Derby was playing poker. Every night we had off, someone was designated to hold the poker game in his or her room. These games usually had a twenty-five-cent ante with a one-dollar bet up to a maximum of three dollars. However, there were times when we would increase the ante and maximum. My wife came from a family of ten children, and it was a ritual for the adults to play cards on the weekends while the children watched. In Francine's case, she watched carefully, learning how to bet and play a hand. I made the mistake of playing poker with her. I thought I was teaching her, but she taught me. Thanks to Francine, we always had extra money, as she seldom lost.

When the Roller Derby teams were sold to Bill Griffith and teams started traveling by bus, the teams played poker every day on the bus ride to a new city. Again, Francine would clean up. On days off, everyone played more poker. Francine and I would usually go out for an expensive dinner and a movie before she would head off to the card game while I watched TV or read. Francine would clean up before the night was over.

Jerry the Kahuna

Between 1968 and 1970, we had a fun-loving, joke-playing, hardworking infield trainer by the name of Jerry "the Kahuna" Witch Doctor. He was from the Hawaiian Islands and knew a little about medicine and physical therapy, and he was a great guy who made everyone happy to be around him. He could apply a Band-Aid or butterfly bandage for a serious cut until you could get to a doctor. He learned how to tape up ankles and shins to help with shin splints. He could massage out a charley horse or cramp. But mostly, he was good at helping fallen skaters and picking up girls in the audience. He was always there when we needed him, and he taught us how to cook a chicken using an electric frying pan, butter, and beer. The problem was that the frying pan would blow most fuses at the Holiday Inns we stayed at, resulting in management outlawing any cooking in the rooms.

Jerry was a good baseball and football player and did well in our road-trip games. He could not skate. He tried a few times, but he couldn't get the knack of it. His wife and kids seldom came to games and were always in the background. Many of us didn't know he was married until he had worked with us for a few months. It's funny how many lives the Roller Derby touched, but we were so wrapped up in our own lives that we didn't even notice the support staff that held all of this together.

Granby, Quebec

Francine and I were based in Montreal, Francine's birthplace and hometown, in 1967. We had developed two teams out of the training school, and we were on our own mini–road trip with one-night stands at different small towns outside Montreal. This particular story took place only eighty-five miles from Montreal. That day, in May, the morning temperature was in the sixties, and by noon, it had dropped to 50 degrees and was heading lower, with snow expected by game time. That's right—the temperature went from the sixties and clear skies to snow in less than twelve hours.

I got on the phone and, with the help of the staff from Mr. O.'s office, started calling my skaters and track crew to tell them to get on the road to Granby as soon as possible. The trip was a joy. The road ran parallel to the Saint Lawrence Seaway, and the trees were just beginning to bloom along the turnpike. There were eight tollbooths, one for each county the turnpike went through, which meant we had to stop at a tollbooth and pay our toll eight times in eighty-five miles. When we arrived in Granby, it was already getting cold and dark as my track crew got ready to set up. The skaters followed in a couple of hours. With any luck, the skaters and fans would get to the arena in time for the big show.

By the time the game started at eight o'clock that night, the little ice-hockey arena was sold out, and fans were yelling and screaming in the stands. They'd had to travel through the snow and black ice, slipping and sliding on the roadways, to get there. After driving with those road conditions, they were ready to see great skating and fighting. The game was a good one, and the Fleur De Lys beat the Toronto Tigers. The fans left the arena and began their drives home, and the skaters showered and got ready to travel back to Montreal. Norman made the decision that it was too dangerous to be out on the highway, and he booked us rooms in a nearby ski lodge for the night.

While loading the pieces of track into our semitrailer, I slipped and fell, striking my head against a piece of track and slicing a large gash above my right ear. I was bleeding like a punctured watermelon, and everyone was telling me to get to a nearby clinic where an emergency nurse and doctor attended to the sick and injured. I chose to finish tearing down the track since I was the only one with experience and the crew was new. I walked around shouting orders while holding a towel to my wound until the job was done.

After a shower and quick tape job, I headed to the lodge with everyone else and began to drink myself silly. The bleeding wouldn't stop, so they finally convinced me to go to the clinic for help. When we arrived, the nurse took down my info, and then the doctor took a quick look at my injury and told me to sit down and wait. After what seemed like an hour or two, with the alcohol wearing off, my head was pounding, and I wanted to know when the doctor was going to take care of me.

When we'd first walked in, we'd noticed that one of the two exam rooms had a male patient on a table covered with a blood-soaked sheet. The doctor and nurse were working feverishly on the young man. When I started to protest about the poor service, the doctor turned to me and said in a stern voice that he was trying to save the young man's life. This young man had been in a terrible accident, and they were working to stabilize him as they waited for the ambulance that would take him to a regular hospital. My injuries were minor, and I wouldn't bleed to death. I might even sober up. I humbly sat down and kept my mouth shut until they could care for me.

Unfortunately, the young man did not make it to the hospital. After a few more minutes, the doctor came in and cleaned my wound, shaved the side of my head, and then proceeded to sew up the gash. Driving back to the lodge, I realized that a cut in the head and a few stitches were not a big deal. At least I would continue to live, drink, laugh, and love. That young man no longer had those opportunities. His family would have to live with the loss, and he would never get to do all the things I would probably take for granted.

RETIREMENT FROM THE ROLLER DERBY

As I begin to write about facing retirement from the Roller Derby, I need to share information from an e-mail I received from Bill Accord concerning the funeral for Jo Jo Stafford, which was recently held at Travis Air Force Base, outside of Sacramento, California. It was a military funeral with ten soldiers: one to play taps; six to act as pallbearers; and three to do the gun salute. I never knew Jo Jo was in the service, nor did I know he had a son living in Australia. His son, Joe Jr., traveled to the States for the service and to visit with his stepmother, Darlene. Jo Jo had many friends with their own stories, which I hope will be told.

When Francine and I left the Roller Games in Winnipeg, we thought we were leaving forever, and it would have been that way if not for Don Drewry and Mike Gammon getting us together for four games in 1975. We played one game each in Chicago, New York, Dallas, and San Jose. We were so out of shape after two years of the good life that the games were not up to the standards we had hoped for. Time is relentless on your body and your will. We all skated hard, and when the whistle blew, I knew it was my last game.

My Realtor, Joe Annunziato, contacted me when he heard that Francine and I were back at home. He convinced me to get my real-estate license and go to work for him. While studying for eight weeks, I did carpenter and painting jobs on the side and worked on our own home. I thought this new career was going to be fun. Every time I saw Joe, he was driving a big, new car; he played tennis at the club five to six days a week; and he always ate at the best restaurants in town. I wanted the life I thought he had. I convinced Francine that all would be well. After all, we had our profit sharing, and that was like a year's pay sitting in our bank account.

I passed my real-estate exam on the first try, which I thought was normal until I found out later that there is only a 50 percent pass rate. I'm glad I wasn't aware of that statistic, or I might not have done so well. Quickly, I found out that real-estate sales were hard work. It is a seven-day-and-night-a-week job, and you rack up a lot of expenses every month. Given the overhead and our lack of income, it didn't take long for the job to eat up our savings. In the six months after my initial start, I was back to working as a carpenter five days a week, and I worked nights and weekends in real estate to close a few sales. It wasn't until the 1975 games that I saw the handwriting on the wall. My Roller Derby days were over, and I knew I'd better start doing all the things that I hated but knew were necessary to do the sales job fully and properly in order to build my real-estate business. This meant knocking on doors and talking to people about real estate, something most people enjoy. In those days, you could still use the telephone to make cold calls in the evenings to talk to prospective buyers and sellers. When the National Do Not Call Registry came into play, we were no longer allowed to do that. It amazes me that politicians are still allowed to do it, but regular folks trying to earn a living or build a business are prohibited from this form of free speech. As you can tell, I have a few gripes with our government and some of its policies.

Francine and I had a hard time not only financially but also with our new lives as regular people. It wasn't long before Francine went back to skating in more games from 1975 to 1980. I stuck to my guns and developed my business. Today I don't regret it. The market might be tough, but through the grace of God and our friends, I made a decent living. I miss the Roller Derby more than almost anything in my life. It is hard for me to express how much I loved skating and working in the Roller Derby. The lifestyle fit me, and I was proud of what we did and how we did it. There isn't a day that goes by that I don't think about some aspect of the derby, and with my efforts to write this book, I find myself tearing up occasionally when I recall some of the people and good times we had while hopping across the United States and Canada. My God, what a life! I have no regrets.

The pressure that came with changing our lifestyle and adjusting to my new career, which was demanding and had me working eighteen hours a day seven days a week, took a toll on me and on our marriage. Within a couple of years, I found myself looking at other women and tasting the forbidden fruit: I started having affairs. Francine and I went through two years of counseling and rebuilt our marriage for a while. During that time, I was faithful and honest to her and our marriage. Our son, Charles Anthony, was born in 1977, and our daughter, Jacqueline, was born in 1982. I tried to make the relationship work, but I blew it. In 1984, I admitted to Francine that I was having an affair and wanted a divorce. I moved in with the other woman, and we eventually married in 1990, only to divorce in 1991.

During the period of 1988 through 2006, I never followed the Roller Derby, hung around the old gang, or attended a Roller Derby member's funeral. I didn't have anything to do with the Roller Derby. I was done, and the memory of the derby life was history I did not plan to relive. Francine and I remained friends and shared joint custody while raising our two children. Francine married a great guy who is now a personal friend of mine, Steve Lopez. They continue their lives in Mountain House, California. Charlie; his wife, Christy; and their daughter, Zoey, live with Francine, while Jacqueline moved back in with me. She graduated with honors from the University of the Pacific in Stockton with a degree in business administration, and she works in Pleasanton, California. Charlie works for Lowes Hardware Company. Christy, Charlie's wife, is expecting their second child. Their eight-year-old, Zoey, is anxious for the new member of their family to arrive.

Diane, my love for the last fourteen years, with help from Francine, convinced me to attend a Roller Derby reunion in Richmond, California, last November. It changed my life. Many of my old friends were there and were happy to see me. We talked story, as the Hawaiians say. I reconnected with many of them as I worked on this book, if only for my own well-being. I want the story to be told and to be shared for what it is—a part of American history. Hundreds of lives were affected by the pursuit of becoming Roller Derby stars, and for those of us lucky enough to have experienced it, if even for a brief time, the experience enriched our lives and our appreciation for the country we live in. Whether people shared the adventure for only a few months or for years doesn't matter. We were the Roller Derby.

SCUBA-DIVING DAYS

December 7, 1941, was "a day that will live in infamy." Seventy-three years later, we still remember that dreadful day in Hawaii when the Japanese attacked Pearl Harbor and the United States of America officially entered World War II. Today I think about all the destruction and loss of life and peace. I think about the goals I had that revolved around diving among the shipwrecks of the war. I once dove on the USS *Blue Gill*. Commissioned in 1939, she was designed as an attack submarine. When we went to war with Japan, she was recommissioned with orders to sink Japanese ships.

In 1971, long after the war had ended, she was stripped of all valuables: brass, instruments, engines, and the beautiful teakwood slats that made up her deck. She was then scuttled in the harbor between Maui and the island of Lanai. The USS *Blue Gill* was sunk about a mile off the coast of Maui, near the city of Lahaina, in about 120 to 150 feet of water, after which navy divers used her for training purposes. The stern came to rest at a depth of 150 feet, with the bow at 120 feet because of the slope of the ocean floor.

In 1978, a full year in advance, I made my reservations to dive on the submarine. The ship was only available for public dives consisting of a six-man group on Thursday afternoons. That was why I had to book so far in advance. You can imagine the rush I felt when I learned that I had been accepted on the dive, provided I finished my open-water NAUI certification three months in advance of the dive. Our vacation was scheduled for September 1 through September 21, 1979. I had the dive planned for September 10.

When we arrived in Maui, I planned to dive that afternoon. It would be a shallow dive because of the plane trip. I'd planned two tank dives for the next seven or eight days in order to get my skill level and confidence up. Up until then, I'd done all my diving along the California coast and in Monterey Bay. I was concerned about my upcoming dive, as the deepest I had ever gone was about 120 feet, and I'd done that only one time. Most of my other dives had been in water that was between thirty-five and forty-five feet. This was going to be a bounce dive. We would only have about five or six minutes of bottom time, and we were using one single seventy-two-cubic-foot tank.

The day of the dive, I did my usual eight-mile run in the morning, snorkeled for about an hour, and grabbed some rest before driving to Lahaina, Maui, to catch the boat out to the sub. There were six of us, seven counting the dive master. The trip out to the dive spot took only about fifteen minutes, which was just enough time to check our gear and get a briefing from our dive master. We looked at photos of the sub while the dive master told us where we would enter and what route we would take once we were at the sub. The small boat we were in was a reconditioned fishing boat with a small cabin for the captain and his one-man crew. Our tanks and gear were stored in the aft section on deck with a canopy overhead to shield us from the intense sun.

The dive master used a photo of the sub to show us how we would approach it, starting at the conning tower, working toward the aft section near the rear torpedo area, proceeding over the side of the sub, and working our way back toward the conning tower. Once there, we would move toward the bow before turning back toward the conning tower, ascending as we swam back. We were scheduled to do three brief decompression stops: one at thirty feet, another at twenty feet, and the last at ten feet. This would allow our bodies to purge all the trapped nitrogen and prevent us from getting nitrogen narcosis (the bends). It all sounded like fun, and we were anxious to get in the water.

While checking my gear, I noticed that my tank only showed 2,200 psi instead of the normal 3,000 psi. The dive master said I shouldn't worry about the gauge on the tank. The reading was incorrect, and since I was the senior diver in the party, I could handle it should it become a problem. I should have insisted on another tank, but I didn't.

We put on our gear, went through a review briefing, and then hit the water, descending to the sub. The water was fairly clear with a little current, so we used the anchor line down to the sub. At fifty feet or so, we could make out the ghostly outline of the sub. The water seemed to become clearer the more we descended. The distance from the anchor line to the sub was about thirty yards, so we let go of the line and swam toward the conning tower. Once there, we all checked our pressure gauges; mine showed only 700 psi, while the others had 1,000 to 1,200 psi. I was concerned and showed my gauge to the dive master. He just waved me off, giving me the okay sign. So I continued the dive with the others, stopping to take photos at regular intervals. As we returned back toward the conning tower, before starting toward the bow, I took another look at my pressure gauge, and it was down to 300 psi, in the red zone. Not a good thing! I showed my dive buddy, and I pointed up as I swam alongside the conning tower. Just as I got even with the tower, about ninety feet from the surface, I took my last breath of air and felt the awful feeling of sucking my tank dry.

At a time like that, it is hard to keep from panicking, but I had been trained and knew what I had to do. One of the toughest things to do is to blow out the air you have in your lungs when your body is screaming for more air. I started swimming toward the surface and let out small breaths of air as I swam. I was thinking about dying, and I saw Francine and my relatives surrounding my casket, as crazy as it sounds. I thought about hanging on to my seven-pound camera and strobe light, and I fought the impulse to just swim up as fast as I could. I knew that would mean the bends and almost certain death. I continued to rise and felt myself beginning to get dizzy and lightheaded. I thought I wasn't going to make it to the surface without blacking out.

I was praying, and I heard a spiritual voice remind me that air expands as you rise; therefore, I knew there could be a residual breath or two in my tank. I tried taking in a breath, and the air was there. I took another full breath, and the tank went dry again. But it was enough to get me to the top. I wouldn't be able to decompress, but I would take my chances.

As I broke through the surface, I realized I had been coming up faster than I had intended. The deckhand on board our little boat yelled out at me, "Are you okay?" He knew I had come up too fast, and the other divers were not with me. He threw me a line and pulled me in. I was exhausted and had a difficult time getting out of the water and back on board the boat. By this time, the other divers were popping up and swimming toward the boat. When the dive master made it to the surface, he looked mad. When he got on board, he started to chew me out, but once he saw my tank gauge and realized he had put my life in jeopardy because he hadn't wanted to take the time to change my tank, he calmed down and asked me what had happened.

When you dive, especially in waters or circumstances that are new to you, you must have a dive partner in case of emergencies like this one. My dive partner should have followed me up and shared his air with me—they call it buddy breathing. You alternate taking in air from your buddy's tank while working your way toward the surface, taking time to decompress, and then you both walk away from the dive. I was lucky to have survived this dive and even luckier to not have gotten the bends. I did have sore muscles and joints for a few days, which are signs of trapped nitrogen bubbles.

I took it easy for the rest of our trip and didn't scuba for a couple of months after getting home. I kept my camera, and I have some great shots of the sub, including one I liked so much that I had it enlarged.

I took it as we left the anchor line to swim toward the sub. Every time I look at it, I remember how God was there. He reminded me to take another breath, and he provided me the will to live and the knowledge to take my time.

Another of my diving adventures involved Cliff Butler. He and I decided to dive Salt Point Ranch, California. This area along the Northern California coast is about a three-and-a-half-hour drive from San Francisco. Cliff and I convinced our wives that this would be a great way to spend our Thanksgiving, so after renting a canvas six-man tent, a Coleman stove, four cots, and a lantern and packing our dive gear and camping stuff, we headed for Santa Rosa and then went up the coast.

It was late Wednesday when we finally got on the road. We were not the only ones getting out of town. After all, this was Thanksgiving weekend, and everyone was heading out of town. We were in traffic all the way to Santa Rosa and through Jenner, where we turned onto the coastal highway to drive to Salt Point Ranch. As an added bonus, it started to rain as soon as we hit the coastal road.

Now, picture this: we pulled into the campground, which was really a dirt road with turnouts and picnic tables under some pine trees. The area was hilly and muddy, with few flat spots. We found a suitable spot to park our two cars and make camp, getting as close to the ocean as possible. It was now dark, and we used the headlights from the cars to give us enough light to pitch our tent. Let me say right here that neither Cliff nor I were ever taught how to camp, and our wives were even less help.

The rain was really coming down, and we were in the dark, trying to get this tent erected. The girls went back to one of the cars and watched us do our manly thing. Cliff and I finally got the tent set up. We moved the lantern and stove into the tent. We decided we would cook inside the tent to avoid the rain. We had one problem: there was no vent other than the front flap of the tent, and it was facing the oncoming wind.

We are real men of genius. The rain lightened up, so we moved the stove and lantern outside. I become the chef, trying to fry potatoes and pork chops and heat up some beans. The girls made salad, and Cliff kept me supplied with beer.

We were so hungry that everything tasted great. We had our meal inside the tent, so we were dry and a little warmer. We all had a good laugh about our camping experience. By the time we finished our meal, the rain had completely stopped. The moon came out, and it was beautiful. We could hear the ocean, and we took our lantern and flashlight and headed toward the sound of the surf hitting against the rocks. Even in the dark, with only moonlight bouncing off the ocean, we could see the whitecaps, and when we heard the pounding surf, we realized that our dive plans might have to change.

We followed the muddy dirt road down to the boat-launch area, and there we saw and heard the power of the ocean. This was a big storm, and the likelihood of our dive day being a safe one was slim to none. After a few minutes of standing in the blowing wind, we headed back to the comfort of our tent. When we got back to the tent, we realized we should have tied the tent down in order to keep it from blowing away. I was glad I had included extra rope and two extra plastic tarps with our camping gear.

Then the fun began. We started opening up our canvas army cots. The six-man tent was only big enough for six men if you slept on the floor in a cozy position. With the four cots open, we were side by side and touching the wall of the tent. You never want to tough the side of a tent when it is raining, as anything that touches the walls of the tent will draw in the rainwater. That meant we would all be wet, our sleeping bags would be wet, and we would be miserable and cold.

I took one of the extra tarps and some rope and made a pup tent over Francine and me by tying a rope from the front of the tent pole to a tree about seven feet away and then draping the tarp over the rope. Then I placed pegs down the sides of the tarp and hammered them into the soft, muddy ground. This allowed us to keep the tent door open and position two bunks partly inside the tent and the rest under the tarp. The only problem was that when someone needed to go potty, Francine and I would have to move out of the way, but this arrangement would work for now.

The next morning, while the girls made breakfast, Cliff and I walked down to view the wave action. It was still stormy, and the waves were pounding the rocks. We could see that this would not be a day to dive. Not to worry—we had brought board games, playing cards, and our radio, and we all liked to hike, especially at the ocean. We spent most of the day walking on the beaches, hiking the trails, and thanking God for our good favor.

We had brought some T-bone steaks for our Thanksgiving feast, and I dug a pit to make baked potatoes. We also had corn on the cob and green beans. This time, we were able to cook our feast in the afternoon sunshine, and we had two—okay, four—bottles of wine and lots of beer. We drank, ate, sang, and laughed our way through another day.

On Friday, Cliff and I decided we would go out spearfishing for our dinner and maybe get some abalone as well. We could use scuba tanks to spearfish, but we would need to free dive without tanks in order to legally get abalone. Our plan was to find where the abalone were plentiful while spearfishing. We would then to go back in and get some abalone. It was a great plan, but the ocean had something different in mind.

The ocean was pounding in, and the waves were seven to eight feet high as Cliff and I entered the water at the boat-ramp area. The kelp was thick, and the water visibility was about one to two feet—unsafe to dive in. We thought that if we could get out past the kelp beds, the water would be deeper and clearer.

Cliff and I walked as far as we could into the surf and then began swimming out toward the deeper water. The kelp was so thick that my speargun kept getting caught in it. Cliff had left his speargun with his wife on the beach. Apparently, I would be the only hunter that day. We continued to swim for about half an hour and made it to the edge of the kelp beds. The water was a bit calmer away from the surf and the waves. Unfortunately, we were both fatigued by this time and realized we would have to fight the currents and surf in order to get back to the safety of the beach.

We spent maybe ten minutes looking for suitable fish to spear and noticed some abalone. I took a couple of shots at some reef fish and missed badly. We were both really tired and knew it was time to get back in. The current was getting stronger, and the swells were getting bigger. We decided to swim along the bottom as far as we could in order to avoid the thick kelp. Kelp grows like a giant redwood, with a long trunk and thick branches that spread out on the surface, making a thick bed of seaweed that is hard to get through. We talked about the risks and decided this would be the safest way for us to get back.

Cliff and I dove to the bottom as I set my compass, and we headed toward the boat landing. The water was beginning to boil, and at times, the waves would flip us over and over and then throw us against the rocks. Just as we were getting to the area where the waves were breaking, I saw a large lingcod about twenty to twenty-five inches long sitting on a rock, and without thinking, I took the shot and got him in the sweet spot: right between the eyes. His mouth flew open, and he arched as he died. I pulled him in, grabbing him by the gills. Holding the speargun, the line, and the fish, I followed Cliff through the surf.

I could feel the ocean current building as the water rushed under me, and a big wave pushed me in toward the beach. I lost sight of Cliff and was worried he might have been caught in the kelp—or worse. I had no choice but to swim as hard as I could and let the wave take me in to safety. As the wave broke over me, I began to feel the water pulling from underneath me, so I dug my hands, my speargun with the fish, and my knees into the sand—a method I learned at Monastery Beach in Carmel, California. I held on till the next wave broke over me, and then I used the energy of that wave to push farther toward the beach. I did this about three or four times before I was out of the main surf. At that moment, I felt my friend Cliff reaching down and helping me to safety. He had made it safely in and was able to take the speargun and fish from me. I was so tired that I don't know if I could have made it out of the water without Cliff's help.

We didn't go back in that afternoon for abalone, even though we knew where they were.

It would have been suicide. We had lingcod for dinner, one of the finest-tasting ocean fish in the California coastal area. We had another day and night of laughter, song, and games.

On Saturday, after watching the movement of the ocean, we realized the weather was going to get worse, and it was starting to rain. We decided to break camp and head home to a great dinner out at one of our favorite restaurants, Spanger's in Berkeley; a warm house; and a warm bed.

After we broke down the tent and loaded all our gear into the cars, we started to drive out of the area. The rain made the roads muddy and slippery. Cliff drove over a large tree root near our campsite, and his car high-centered on the root. His back wheels were not even touching the ground. He was stuck big-time. There were no gas stations within fifteen miles of where we were camping. No tow trucks or four-wheel-drive pickups were available to help us, so we hooked up ropes to my rear axle and then attached the rope to his front bumper. I tried to haul him off the high-center root.

After only a couple of tugs, I realized I was sliding on the muddy road. I was not getting the traction needed to move Cliff's car. We convinced the girls to sit on the trunk of his car while I pulled with my car. That helped his rear-drive wheel to touch the ground and gave him the traction needed to break free. As his car moved, the girls slid off the trunk and ran to their respective cars. The trip home was uneventful, and the traffic was light until we got to Santa Rosa. That was when we decided to stop and have a good meal before driving the rest of the way home.

Each car switched drivers, and our wives drove. Cliff and I were tired, and we both knew we had taken a stupid chance by going into the roiling sea. I believe it was only through God's grace that we survived. Recently, the newspaper had a story about a diver drowning at Salt Point Ranch. That could have been one or both of us.

Another diving adventure with a little less drama happened when Cliff and I were diving in Monterey at the breakwater, which was a part of the Cannery Row area made famous by John Steinbeck's novel of the same name. Cliff and I enjoyed diving there since it was less than two hours from home. The water entry was usually simple, and sometimes the sea would be a bit rough. If it got too bad, we just went to the wharf or dove at some other spot by Carmel.

This particular day, in the late fall during the 1960s, the weather was mild, with bright sunshine and clear skies. We planned on spearfishing our limit since the fish were plentiful. We wanted to have a fish fry at my house the next day, and we planned to invite Bill and Dee Morrissey and Don Drewry. The swim out was relaxed, as the wave action was mild, and there was little surge to contend with. Even the kelp beds were easy to navigate through on that particular day.

When we reached a large clear area in the kelp bed, we knew we were over a rock reef with the bottom about thirty feet down. This was a spot we had fished before with great results. The only thing we needed to worry about were the sea lions that would steal our fish. I made a float out of an inner tube and two pieces of quarter-inch plywood tied together. One piece had a trapdoor forming the top, and the other formed the bottom. We had a five-pound weight tied to the float with a quarter-inch rope, and we let it drop to the bottom. It acted like an anchor. This way, as we shot our fish, we could swim to the surface and place the fish inside the hole formed by the inner tube and the plywood. Today they make similar devices out of nylon tarps. I should have patented the idea.

Cliff and I did the mandatory check of each other's equipment, and with a thumbs-up, we dove down to the bottom to begin our search for legal-sized fish. Monterey Bay was full of fish back in the 1960s, and we did our part to reduce their numbers. However, we only harvested what we could eat and never killed fish for sport. I believe the depletion of fish in this area was caused by water pollution. On a dive we took a few months earlier, Cliff and I came out of the water after a dive and saw one of the City of Monterey's road-oil trucks dumping unused road oil into the bay and then hosing out the residue from the truck into the bay. We asked the driver what he was doing. He told us to eff off. We called the police and reported the incident, but nothing happened as far as we know.

Cliff and I shot a couple of fish and took them up to the float. Then we went back down. Before reaching the bottom, Cliff stopped to peer into a hole—a small cave in the rocks. Then he backed away quickly. When you are underwater, it can be a little awkward to communicate, and normally, you rely on basic sign language to get your point across. Well, Cliff held up his hand and made what appeared to be an okay signal for me to take the shot. Apparently, there was a good-sized fish in the hole, so I squared up over the hole and saw the big head of the fish—maybe a lingcod, which is the best, tastiest fish in the bay. I thought it was nice of Cliff to let me spear this one.

I lined up my shot and positioned my feet to brace myself against the rocks as I pulled the trigger on my double-band Arbalete speargun. The arrow shot out and found its mark, hitting the fish. It immediately swam back into the hole, pulling the spear and my gun into the hole. Fortunately, I had my feet braced against the rocks, with both hands pulling on the gun and the end of the spear. Suddenly, the fish came out of the hole, and to my surprise, it was a wolf eel. It was about three feet long but looked like one about six feet long. It was swimming right toward my stomach with its mouth open, bearing its teeth. I knew if it bit me, I would be in serious trouble. I hung on to the end of the spear and was able to keep the eel at bay. It continued to swim back and forth, trying to take a bite out of one of us. It was time to head to the surface.

Just as we broke through the surface, the irritated eel went limp, as I had seen other fish do when they died. I carefully grabbed the head of the eel and removed the spearpoint from the shaft. I slid the spear out of its body and prepared to place it in the inner-tube compartment. Cliff was holding the trapdoor open, when the eel jumped out of my hand and into the water. We both swam in opposite directions, hoping to see the eel while avoiding its attack. Neither of us saw that pissed-off eel again. We decided to swim back to the beach and shoot any fish we saw.

When we were safely out of the water, we took off our masks, and I asked Cliff about his signal with the index finger and thumb almost touching to form an okay sign. He told me I had misunderstood. The sign he had given me was the sign for big teeth. I suggested in a calm voice that next time, he should close his fist tightly with only the middle finger stuck out to inform me that it was not a good idea to take a shot.

We both laughed and gave each other a manly shove. Then it was time to wash the gear, clean the fish, and have a couple of beers before heading to the wharf for a hot shower and some hot food.

I have many other memorable diving stories, but those were the best. I miss diving with my friend. I have lots of memories and photos of our sea-hunt days. Recently, I got an e-mail from Cliff, who now lives in Santa Barbara, asking me to join him and some other friends and skaters in a couple of weeks in San Francisco for pizza, beer, and stories.

Another diving adventure was with Dave Cannella, one of our truck drivers and referees. Dave tried out for skating, but he was better suited as a referee and was a great truck driver. During the off-season, Dave and I did a little scuba diving, but Dave had done all his previous diving in Florida, at Pennekamp State Underwater Park. The water was warm and clear compared to the 57-degree Monterey water, where the visibility on a great day is thirty feet, rather than Florida's hundred-foot visibility. Needless to say, for Dave to get into a three-eighths-inch-thick wet suit, carry twenty-four pounds of lead weight to compensate for the buoyancy, and then enter water with only ten- to fifteen-foot visibility on average was hard. He didn't like it, but he was a good sport, and we did a few dives together.

Dave had the idea to build underwater housing for my Super 8 movie camera out of Plexiglas. It took about two weeks to build the prototype. Then we went to the breakwater at Monterey Bay, and since I was the senior diver, I got to try it out. The water visibility wasn't too bad— about eighteen feet. We had a lot of ambient light, which was great since we didn't have a strobe or flash. Unfortunately, the shots were dark even when taken at shallow depths. The picture clarity was poor due to the camera autoadjusting for the density of the water. It was okay. We didn't know what the heck we were doing, but we had fun testing it and dreaming of mass-producing our underwater housing. However, before the Warren Buffett in us took over, we were back on the road again.

During the camera trials, Mike Gammon hooked up with Dave and me with his six-man rubber raft. In the past, we'd always swum out to where we planned to dive in order to save our precious air supply. The idea of having a raft to carry us out to our favorite dive spots seemed like a great idea. The first problem we had was paddling our way out to the dive spot; it was just as exhausting as swimming. The second problem we encountered was that the inflatable sections of the raft were tall. It proved impossible to get back into the raft without first taking off our diving gear and throwing it into the raft.

We only used the raft about half a dozen times before my good friend Larry, a mechanic and my coworker at the Wayne Campbell's Mobile station, joined us in diving. He had a six-man raft with an outboard motor and a wooden bottom. That was great—we could pump it up, place the wood bottom sections in, attach the outboard motor, and be on our way in less than ten minutes. It had low gunwales, which made it much easier to get in and out of. Plus, if the visibility was bad in one area, we could simply motor to another spot and make our dive.

MIKE YOHNICKI'S MEMORIES

Hi, Mike and Michelle,

Thank you for the reply and all the stories. I printed your e-mail out to read again. Diane and I just got back from a motor-home trip to Santa Cruz, California. I will write you more over the weekend. Got to catch up for all those days away.

God bless you,

Larry

That sounds relaxing for some reason. I miss Rancho Mirage/Palm Springs. Let me know, as I was somewhat in a hurry trying to remember some of the highlights.

Mike

First chance to get near this thing since coming home from the hospital. Who would have thought that I would be minus a leg now? I guess that will end any skating! Everyone says I look a lot better. I think that somewhere in December, I will be in a rehab hospital, getting a new leg. I asked for a bionic one, but they ran out. I did, however, read the book sections that you sent

Michelle while I was in the hospital. Fascinating! I can relate to your dad in those early years. When we came to London for games, the cheering on was from my grandparents, who raised me. My dad was a successful garage and gas-station owner in Winnipeg. However, he also was a huge drunk. I think he had a revolving door at the city jail. Thus, I never really knew him, and as for my mother, I never saw or knew her after I was three months old. I guess they gave me to my grandparents.

Now, as far as the Sudbury cold night, you left out that damn ramp to the arena floor from the outside. That was a killer run. But thinking of cold, remember Chicoutimi, where it was minus 40 degrees? We were in the van on the way to Quebec City—me, you, Doug Dyer, Dave Bate, Sal, and Peter Kelly rode the bus. I was a real gentleman (ha) and gave up my seat to Francine so she could sleep. I slept on the skate bags in the back, but it was still cold. We stopped at a truck stop to grab some hot food, but I will say, you sure did a lot of hours driving.

The Toronto Game

Remember after the Toronto game finished, when we headed out with Super Clutch behind the transport wheel? Cox and Dave Bate rode with him, and I followed in the van. I noted that up the highway, there was a fire in the median. As we got closer, it turned out to be our truck. It had been hit by a small car. Our guys went to the hospital. It turned out okay for all. You spoke about Sal; what a guy! He and this saying: "JIGGY JAGGY." Barry Dale, one of two announcers, last I heard worked at a pizza shop or owned it in Kingston, and Aaron Rand, the other guy, became a radio DJ in Montreal. I want to mention also after the game in Stratford,

Ontario. Griffith came up from Los Angeles, and all of you American skaters were in the dressing room. Griffith announced those drastic pay cuts. Boy, did we have a lot of skaters wanting to work track crew.

Deceit

Remember in 1974, when you and Francine were to head to San Francisco to do some Bombers? I think it was Pioneers or Jolters games. So Francine had to look as if Charlie Mitchell broke her leg, and you hit the ref to get tossed from the series. So on the tour, you hit Seattle, and a Canadian fan from Vancouver saw the afternoon TV game of the episode only to see you and her skating. He asked that question, how come Francine is skating when he was the Canadian game. Yup—taped months ago!

And yes, Mr. O was pretty cheap. Vancouver game day, I asked him for a few extra bucks. I did not know that Doug and Barry had done so too. You saved our bacon, or at least mine. I kind of wondered that night while taking the track down. Mr. O tried to slip a young girl who wanted to try out on the track, and you were not having any part of it, having her get off the track. So I know you were very ticked off. It kind of was a letdown in Winnipeg, as we were headed back from our tour, that you two were heading home. It felt like I lost two good friends, but I also know what you meant about Derby and Roller Games. I guess being there, I just did not focus on the differences very much. Though I was really surprised that Bob Heinz asked me if I would help with a training camp on the West Coast. I realized that was for the 1975 attempt at the Madison Square Garden's game that some of you did with Heinz, O'Connell, Weston, Cavallo, etc. I have a video of that game.

More Mike Memories

I also want to thank you for the years of keeping in touch. I might as well say that now, since if I did not have the leg taken, I cut it pretty close to not being here today. If I could turn the clock back, I would to that time. I think I was very happy being a part of the sport (though someday you guys may think otherwise). I took the job very seriously, so if I didn't chuckle a lot, sorry. I can say, other than the railroad as my first love, that compared to any other job I have tackled over the years. I was happy most with the derby and the railroad. I met a lot of great people, different in their own way. Some I have kept in touch with, and with my large collection, over the years, I have, like you guys, sent material to them to pass down to their family. I will be going through stuff once I have a new leg. But your book was likely the first in a very long time that I read anything from, and I would like to see the finished product. Most of the material I have was at one time on our website: Roller Derby Preservation Association. It was started to remember the Derby back in the '90s. It did very well, including the ill-fated roller jam a few years ago. The site got hacked twice, and we never restored it. A lot of pictures and stories appeared on it. I have seen Fitzpatrick's attempt of derby, but I have not seen the speedsters like we had back then. And ever with my attempts to bring it back with three TV networks, they didn't seem interested. So much for us has-beens! As long as we remember the game, you can't take that away. I've jabbered on long enough. I should let you get back to work. Say hi to Francine when you see her, and I hope all is well with you.

CLIFF BUTLER, NAUI CERTIFIED

In 1968, Cliff Butler and I became NAUI-certified scuba divers off the coast of Monterey, California. That isn't big news normally, but few divers were black.

As a matter of fact, Cliff was only the second black man to be certified out of Bob Hollis's Anchor Shack in Hayward, California. They were not at all prejudiced there, but it was rare for a black person to come into the Anchor Shack to even ask about certification as a diver. Keep in mind that in 1968, Hollis was training new divers at a rate of twenty-five to thirty per month. They had been doing this for two years. By the way, if you recognize Hollis's name, it might be because he also owns Oceanic Divers, a company that makes diving equipment distributed around the world. He was lead diver for the dive on the *Andrea Doria*, a cruise ship that sank in the Atlantic. Bob and his crew lived on board the ship 250 feet down in a small, cramped three-man sub attached to the deck of the *Andrea Doria*. They were looking for a safe that was rumored to contain a small fortune, but when opened on TV, it only had soaked papers and mud.

Cliff was my diving buddy, and during the Bombers' regular season, we would spend our weekends diving in the Monterey and Carmel areas or up the Northern California coast. We even tried diving for gold in the American River, just upstream from where John Sutter discovered the first gold that started the California gold rush of 1849. We found stuff but never found gold.

During our training, some of the other divers would give Cliff a bad time. He was good-natured about it, but the most-used comment was "Cliff smiles when you're down there," meaning underwater. Cliff's retort was always "Sharks love white meat, so stay out of my way." As I said, there was no prejudice—only guys being guys and times being what they were.

Before we could complete our ocean checkouts, which occurred weeks after our training, we had to go through rigorous first-aid training, which included practicing mouth-to-mouth resuscitation. It was 1968, and the gay thing was just beginning to be of concern to straight men. I must admit it was an issue for me to have to give a man resuscitation, but Cliff was my dive partner, and you take responsibility for your dive buddy. Not knowing how to perform CPR properly could cost one of us our life. So on a Saturday, after spending most of the day on other first-aid situations, the time came for us to practice resuscitation. After receiving a lecture and a short demo from our instructor, it was our turn. They asked Cliff and me to go first, and we did. We both passed the test without incident, and the other guys, including two women in our class, let out sighs of relief. It was no big deal.

The following weekend, Cliff and I went down to Monterey for the first of two ocean checks. The first would be without tanks during the dive, and then we'd use tanks for the second dive. We all gathered at the breakwater near Cannery Row. After some instructions, we swam out about fifty yards past the kelp. Once there, we received more instruction as we practiced flooding our masks and then clearing them. We then learned how to swim through kelp beds. Finally, we took turns practicing a rescue using a fellow diver and learned how to perform resuscitation while towing a drowning victim to shore. Our rescue training took most of the day. We then went to the wharf for a hot meal and cold drinks. During dinner, our instructor finally told the other divers who we were and what we did for a living. Needless to say, our dive mates never looked at us the same after that. They wanted free tickets for the next game, which we happily supplied.

Cliff and I spent nine years as dive partners, and we were constantly paying for it by taking two-tank dives in Monterey Bay and then skating that night. You see, there was an unspoken rule about swimming: you shouldn't do it before a game, because it took so much strength from your legs. If you have ever swum through the kelp beds in Monterey, spent forty-five minutes spearfishing, swum back to shore, and then repeated that same process, you know how wiped out we were. To make matters worse, when Cliff and I were on the Bay Bombers together with Charlie O'Connell, he would make Cliff and me skate every jam. Fortunately, Charlie seldom attended the Monterey games. We finally got Charlie to dive with us in Monterey on a skate day. His father-in-law was a professional deep-sea diver and had taught him the basics.

Cliff and I finally convinced Charlie to go diving with us, but he was reluctant since he only dove in Hawaii with clear, warm water and no need for a heavyweight wet suit, not to mention all the additional weight we carried to compensate for the buoyancy created by the wet suit. With the water temperature at 56 degrees, you can go into hypothermia quickly, and there is no reason to risk it. Additionally, the wet suit keeps you warmer if you drink a lot of coffee before going in and then urinate in the suit during the dive. The warm urine heats up the body because of the trapped liquid in between the suit and your body.

Since I had the most experience, I served as the lead diver. I went over the planned dive with Cliff and Charlie. Just to be safe, since Charlie would be diving under the large kelp beds at the breakwater for the first time, we discussed the plan for keeping in view of one another while allowing the necessity to chase and shoot the fish we selected. We would take turns shooting; that way, we could stay together even given the ten-foot visibility. The depth of the water was twenty-five to thirty feet, but with poor visibility and reduced ambient light due to the large kelp canopy and the cloudy weather, we would need to be diligent in our buddy system.

Above us, floating on the surface, was an inner tube from a car tire with a bottom and top made from quarter-inch plywood. It had a trapdoor on top with a latch in order to keep the sea lions from taking our fish as well as to keep our fish from jumping out. The float was tied to the edge of the kelp canopy. The plan was to take turns shooting fish, and then, after we each had a fish, we would swim up to the float and deposit our fish inside. This was a tried-and-true method Cliff and I had developed after many dives.

Given the cloudy day, the water looked dark and foreboding as we began our swim out to the kelp canopy. As we descended into water familiar to Cliff and me, we did a visual check with Charlie, and he seemed a little anxious, which was understandable. Diving under the canopy is like going into a cave, but you can't see the bottom. The top is all kelp. The sea, at that depth and in that condition, was an eerie green. Charlie gave me a thumbs-up, and we proceeded to the bottom. Once we arrived, the visibility was a little better—about fifteen feet, which, for Monterey Bay, is pretty good. This was in 1968, and the fish were everywhere. Cliff helped Charlie load up his Arbalete speargun and then pointed to some fish for Charlie to shoot. After a couple of shots, he finally hit his prey. Then Cliff loaded his speargun and went after a large lingcod he'd spied while watching Charlie shoot. Cliff got it on the first shot. Then it was my turn. I also had already selected a lingcod of my own, and I went after it and shot it.

With our fish in tow, we ascended to the surface at the edge of the kelp beds. When we broke through the surface, the sun was shining, and the water was a little calmer, which was good since we were fifty yards away from our float. After a short swim, we reached the float, and each of us took the point off our spear in order to slide the shaft through the fish. Then we placed our fish in the float. We gave each other a thumbs-up and started back down—at least we thought we were all going back down.

When we arrived on the bottom, Cliff and I couldn't find Charlie. We started searching for him, and I must say, we were worried. The kelp can be unforgiving. If you get caught in it, your first impulse is to try to rip it off, but that only makes matters worse. The best thing to do is to dive under the canopy since kelp is like a tree. Imagine the branches and leaves on top of the water and the trunk under the water, where you can escape the entangling pieces to find a hole in the canopy and swim to clear water. As I said before, the visibility was limited as well.

Cliff and I used up our air supplies and then started searching for Charlie from the surface, using our snorkels. We were both exhausted and feared we had lost our friend. We swam back to the beach, where we planned on calling the coast guard and the police so that their sea-rescue units could search for his body. When we got back to shore, we went over to his motor home to tell his girlfriend the bad news. When we got there, she opened the door to let us in, and we both could see a freshly showered and dressed Charlie O'Connell, our coach, boss, and friend, sitting at the table with a hot cup of coffee in his hand.

Needless to say, we unloaded on him about the basic rules of letting your dive buddies know if you are going in. The fact is that we could have gotten in trouble ourselves while trying to find him in the kelp forest. Furthermore, if he'd told us he was going in, we could have avoided the anxiety we had gone through and the fatigue we were feeling. Afterward, Cliff and I shut up, stepped down to the beach from the motor home, and walked over to my camper. We grabbed a couple of cold beers and premade sandwiches. Neither Cliff nor I said a word as we ate our food and drank the beer. Both of us washed out our gear and then packed it in the camper. There was not to be a second dive that day.

JEAN KEENON AND FAMILY

Around Thanksgiving, I can't help but think of Jean and Ed Keenon, the family who took me into their home just before Thanksgiving in 1964. I had quit my carpenter's job to travel to Los Angeles for a tryout with the Roller Games, which turned out to be a big waste of time. I had given up my apartment and was nearly out of money. I was forced to sleep in my car until I could save enough money to rent an apartment again. Chris Keenon, Jean and Ed's son, found out about my peril and told his parents. They would not let me leave the training school without agreeing to move into their home and share a bedroom with Chris. They were tenacious, and I was tired of sleeping in my car and taking sponge baths in restrooms.

Jean was the most wonderful, caring, warm, and funny person I had ever met. Her smile would light up any room, and she had a heart as big as Texas. Maybe that is a poor choice of words since she had a damaged heart. She was mother to Chris, twelve; Roberta, eleven; Jean, nineteen; and a son who tragically passed away with heart problems when he was only five.

Ed was like Archie Bunker in a lot of ways. He had a lot of opinions, a big heart and soul, and a stoic manner. He worked as a painter at Macy's and took on side jobs when he could get them. He and Jean met when they both lived in New Jersey, and after getting married, they decided to move out west to California. They had already lost one child and had another who worried them to tears, the younger Jean. She was a rebel, and it was the '60s.

Chris and Roberta were great kids, and Chris wanted to skate. He was a natural and would eventually get his chance at stardom. I was the soon-to-be adopted older brother, and they treated me as if I were one of the family. I loved them, and they took great care of me. I moved in a couple of days before Thanksgiving. Jean and Ed were great cooks, and the food was incredible. We soon fell into a routine in which the family followed me to the training school after work. Chris and I would skate while the family watched. Afterward, they would head home while I met with my friends for a drink or two before going home. *Home*—that word has a great sound, and it felt good to say. I had been on my own for a couple of years, and I missed having a family.

Eventually, I went to Phoenix to skate in the semipro league and then returned home for a few weeks before Bert Wall asked me to go on the road to skate with his team. The morning I left for Denver, Ken Monte pulled up outside the Keenon home to pick me up, and the hugs and kisses went on and on, until finally, Ken said it was time to go in a voice that I knew not to question. In the car, Ken, his wife, and an attractive female skater whose name I can't recall remarked what a great family I had. When I told them the story of the Keenons rescuing me from my car motel, they were almost in tears. Well, at least the women shed a few tears. They couldn't believe how loved I was in such a short time.

For the next couple of years, I would stay with the Keenons when I was in town, and our relationship grew like a family. Since I had lost contact with my own family, this was my home, and they were my family. In 1967, I married Francine, and she and I moved into the Nimitz Motel in San Leandro after finishing a road trip. I went back to work at the Mobile gas station in Hayward, working sixteen-hour shifts seven days a week to support my new family. Francine was alone in the motel all day and finally accepted the Keenons' offer for us to move in with them.

One night, when we had been there for only a couple of weeks, Ed found his loving wife, Jean, sitting at the kitchen table. She had been having a cup of coffee, waiting for me. Every night, she would make a pot of coffee just before I was due to arrive home. She and I would talk and laugh about life over cups of coffee. Francine would come join us most of the time. That night, before I got home, Ed awakened with a terrible feeling in his stomach and decided to check on his wife. She had died with a cup of coffee, which was now spilled on the floor, in her hand. I walked in a couple of minutes after Ed made the discovery. We tried CPR and called 911, but they said she was already gone.

About four weeks later, Francine and I went back on the road. Ed and the kids stayed in the Hayward apartment for a few more years. Francine and I tried to stay in contact when we were in town and through a few cards and phone calls, but after Ed passed away and Roberta and Chris were on their own, we lost the family.

Today I have reestablished contact with Chris and his wife, through Chris's efforts more than mine. Roberta is in Utah with her family and the family of her sister, Jean. Chris and I call one another once in a while, and someday we will all be together again. I can't wait to see Jean's smiling face.

AND GOD WAS THERE!

As I sit at my computer, working on this book, I realize I should really be working on my real-estate business. I should be calling potential clients and working to get more business. The real-estate market is the worst I have seen since 1979–84, when interest rates went from 7 percent to 18 percent and I had to knock on doors for six hours a day six days a week to feed my family. But God was there! He provided for my family and me.

Bob Reinhold, the associate pastor at my church, asked me to give my testimony at a future service after I made this comment to him: "Commission salespeople wake up every day unemployed, and only by the grace of God do we feed our families." John Bruce, our regular pastor, was doing a series on the effectiveness of prayer when we pray for God's glory and not our own. Of course, before giving his request much thought, I said yes. I now have to take time to pray that God will help me share the lessons I have learned over the years with our congregation. As humbled as I am by the idea of doing it, I am excited by the possibilities. My challenge is to tell the tale in a way that will glorify God and not me. So far, I have not given the testimony.

My grandmother and my aunt on my dad's side of the family were constantly taking me to church and seeing to it that I learned about God and followed the path he would want for me. They were from the Pentecostal faith, and my uncle George, my dad's brother, was a minister. He was an old hellfire-and-damnation preacher with tent revivals, yelling, and shouting, and I often heard him translate for someone who was speaking in tongues. As a young boy, I found this scary. My family would see to it that I went to church every night, including on weekends if I was in town.

My father and stepmother were not of the church, nor were my stepsister and stepbrother—quite the contrary. My parents spent many a night in the local bar, and as a result, my dad had a hard time keeping a job, which meant we moved every few months on average. My dad, on many occasions, would come home from the bar at midnight or later and announce to us that we were moving—right then, as soon as we could pack up the car. There would be no good-byes to the neighbors or any transfers from schools. Most often, we had to be quiet to keep the unpaid landlord from finding out we were making a run for it.

Usually, they would drop me off at my grandparents' or my aunt Ruth's place until Dad had settled in a new town and secured employment. So I would get to go to church and to school and have a regular life for a couple of weeks before I was sent for. As I look back on this Gypsy style of life, I realize how often God was there. There were numerous times when the old car we traveled in had worn brakes and tires, or we were short on gas and food money and had to lay over for a few hours while Dad wired relatives for help. Help always came either from relatives or complete strangers who were willing to give us food and gas money. God was there!

When I was in the third grade, we were living in a little two-room courtyard-type unit. At Christmastime, I came down with the mumps. Money was short, and food was scarce. Someone had given my dad a case of split-pea soup for some work he had done, so I ate soup for five straight days. By then, my symptoms were beginning to go away. During this time, my parents were hanging out at the bar just up the street. They told us kids about someone who came in with a gun to shoot a guy he thought was seeing his wife. He mistook my dad for the man and fired the gun at my dad. He missed, and a large friend of my dad's picked up the gunman and threw him through a plate-glass window. I know God was there.

There were several incidents of tires blowing out on our old car, and Dad would somehow manage to keep from hitting other cars or a tree or ending up in a ditch. God was there. One time, my dad and my uncle put an old washing machine up on the tongue of the trailer we were pulling in order to add weight to the front end of the trailer to make it easier to control. But when they found that wasn't working, they stopped alongside the road and, with the help of my stepbrother, lifted a large boulder onto the top of the washer. Now, this was a fine idea, but since the car was so full, I had to lie down above the backseat, against the rear window. When a tire blew out on the two-lane road, we were between two high dirt berms, and the trailer was jackknifing. All I could see was that boulder getting ready to come through the rear window at me. An oncoming car had no place to go, as our car was zigzagging across the roadway. My dad drove the car up the berm. The car settled and lay momentarily against the berm before settling back down on all four wheels as the trailer leveled out. God was there!

There were many other times while I was growing up when we were hungry or sleeping in our car and in despair, and I prayed for God's help. Someone would always show up with a bag of groceries or offer us gas money. I know God was there.

Before my seventeenth birthday, we moved to the outskirts of Alta Vista, near Manhattan, Kansas. We were living in an old farmhouse that had been used to store hay. My dad had a carpenter's job at Fort Riley, and we were doing fairly well. My uncle R. V. and his family were living two miles down the road from us in another old farmhouse. Dad wasn't supposed to be drinking, but he often came in with liquor on his breath and the same old slurred speech. He told us one day that he had a new job in San Francisco, and we were leaving that night.

I was doing well in the little four-room high school in Alta Vista. I was finally getting all the credits I needed to qualify for college. I decided I would not move again until I had graduated high school. When I told my dad, he flew into a rage, grabbed a broom, and broke it across my back. I grabbed it, and he stopped. As I looked into his eyes, I told him I would not move again. Then I ran out the door into the dark, cold Kansas night with only a sweatshirt and jeans. I ran down the dirt road toward my uncle's home, and then a thought hit me: this would be the first place my dad would look for me. So I decided to hide in a ditch until they had left. The temperature was supposed to drop to 28 degrees, according to the TV news. I was afraid of dying, but I had made up my mind. I found some tree branches and leaves to cover myself with, and as the hours dragged on, I could hear my dad driving up and down the road, yelling my name out of the car window. Finally, I saw them leaving, pulling the trailer with them, heading for the main road.

Apparently, they had gone to my uncle's house and warned him that I would probably show up. I did show up at the crack of dawn. I was afraid my uncle's family would not take me in, but they did. I had to work on their farm, including milking the cow and slopping the pigs, and when a grave needed to be dug at the local hundred-year-old cemetery, I was hired to do that as well.

By the way, the night I left home, the temperature only dipped down to 38 degrees. The local weatherman had no explanation for the warmer temperature. I did: God was there.

I finished high school with honors at Alta Vista and was accepted to the University of Kansas at Emporia. I worked during the summer with my uncle as a carpenter, as well as doing farm chores every morning and night. I landed two jobs in Emporia: one at the Litwins Everything to Wear store and the other at a Conoco gas station. Between the two jobs, I could go to college and get by until summer, when I could go back to carpentry work, since it paid more. God was there.

Before I graduated from college, my uncle and his family decided to move back to California, to the San Francisco Bay Area. They asked me if I wanted to move back. I had received an offer of a full-time journeyman carpenter's job in San Francisco. For an eighteen-year-old to get into the union as a journeyman was unheard of, since usually, there was a four-year apprenticeship. You could not start till you were eighteen years old. Since Kansas had a right-to-work law, there was little union influence, but because I had been doing the job since I was twelve years old, my dad and two uncles had signed off on me, and they allowed me to start as a journeyman at $5.75 per hour in 1963. That was great pay; plus, I had medical benefits.

That was the beginning of a period when I strayed from God. I started drinking and carousing. I bought a new hot car and, in only six months, racked up sixteen moving traffic violations, including two drag-racing charges. That last drag race cost me my driver's license for thirty days. I sold my new hot car and started taking the bus and asking friends for rides, and I did a lot of walking and thinking.

When I was twelve years old and we were living in San Bernardino, California, my parents started watching the Roller Games on TV, and I got hooked. I saved up my allowance and bought some clamp-on sidewalk skates. Then I taught myself to skate, and of course, I always told anyone who would listen that someday I would be in the Roller Derby. While working in San Francisco, one of my coworkers came in on a Monday morning looking as if he had been mugged. When I inquired, he told me he had gone to tryouts at the Roller Derby Training Center on 105th Avenue and Edes in Oakland, only a mile from my apartment. That Friday night, I went to the training facility and signed up. Six months later, I was skating semipro for a team in Phoenix, Arizona, for twenty dollars a game, doing two games a week. I got a room at a boardinghouse with the promoter's wrestling team. There were six of us who moved to Phoenix for our shot at stardom. We nearly starved to death. But God was there!

My experience in Phoenix landed me a full-time job with the International Roller Derby League and a spot on the Chicago Pioneers. During my ten years in the Roller Derby, God was there. Numerous times, God intervened to spare me and my friends from severe injuries and possible death.

Traveling from the West Coast on Highway 80 in the north, near Little America, Wyoming, we hit black ice and began to spin around in our Chevy El Camino. It was pitch black except for the headlights of oncoming cars. My good buddy Don Drewry was driving, and lucky for us, he kept his cool until we stopped spinning. I don't know how many times we spun around, but it felt like forever. Don righted the car, managed to stay ahead of the truck bearing down on us, and kept us from going into the oncoming traffic. God was there and kept us safe. I caught myself praying for the first time in a long while, and I must tell you—it felt good.

There would be other times when I caught myself praying because of a life-threatening event, bad weather, or no sleep and too many beers the night before and during our trek to the next city. We averaged four hundred to five hundred miles every night. After a game, I would work with the crew taking the track down and loading it into the semitruck for transport to the next city. After a game, I would have a six-pack or two of beer before heading to the next city. I was not only tired and sleepy but also intoxicated. Many times, I fell asleep while driving, and always, God was there. The only accident I had during the more than seven hundred thousand miles of driving I did with the Roller Derby came after a good night's sleep and no beer.

In late 1973, I quit skating and got my real-estate license. By November, I had a job as a full-time agent with A and F Realtors, just down the street from where I was living at 555 MacArthur Boulevard in San Leandro. Six months later, I was working as a full-time carpenter and part-time Realtor. At that time, I decided that my wife and I needed to get back in touch with a church, and we did. Looking back, I realize that it was God who got me to do the things I needed to do in order to change my life. I became a full-time real-estate agent. The market was tough, and in order to get business, I had to start knocking on doors and cold-calling strangers, asking for business.

I put in a lot of long hours praying, and my business started building up. Soon I was actually making a living. God was there! I made many mistakes and did a lot of backsliding before I really turned my life over to God. I have been baptized three times and have knowingly turned to God several times when I was low. I have divorced twice, filed bankruptcy twice, and been on the street, but when I let God take control, my life changed, and it was always for the better. A Realtor friend once told me something that really hit home with me: "Commission salespeople wake up every day unemployed. Even if they show up to work and spend all day working, they do not get paid! They only get paid when they convince a buyer to buy or a seller to sell. Then they solve all the problems between decision and completion." That is a maxim in real-estate sales.

Every day, I ask God to bring into my life people I can help. It is only through him that I have the opportunity to help them reach their goals and mine. I wake up every day unemployed, and I love it. I see God work miracles with my clients on transactions that shouldn't work but somehow do. Lenders make favorable decisions, and inspection problems, appraisals, and escrow challenges get resolved because I believe God is there. I get the opportunity to offer testimony for clients who become friends, and we share our faith. God is there.

As I write this book, many of my friends have given their testimonies before God, and I have prayed for the strength to tell my story as they have done and to be accepted as a Christian friend first, a father and grandfather second, a brother third, and a Realtor last. God is here! I see him, and I feel him in everything I do. God bless you for reading this book.

Surprise Birthday Party for Larry Smith
Left to right: Denae (daughter's friend), Jacqueline (daughter),
Charles (son), Steve Lopez, and Francine Cochu-Lopez.
Celebrating Larry's 33rd birthday again!

Charles (son)

Really, I am only 33, again.

Really, I am only 33, and holding.

Francine Cochu-Lopez with husband Steve Lopez

Thanks to my family and friends.

Diane Sass with my Roller Derby collage birthday gift.

Diane Sass, my special friend.

Roller Derby 2009 Reunion

*** ALL LEAGUES *** ALL SKATING FAMILY***

February 28, 2009

@

Harry's Hofbrau
390 Saratoga Ave.
San Jose, CA 95129
(408) 243-0434

Happy Hour 4:30 p.m.–5:30 p.m.
Dinner 5:30 p.m.
Festivities and Dance 7:00 p.m.–10:30 p.m.
Includes
Dinner / Dance / T-Shirt / Gift Bag + More

$50.00 advanced by February 1 $65.00 after February 2
$75.00 @ door night of the banquet if available

Tickets may be ordered by mailing check or money order made out to ARSD to

Delores Tucker	Georgia Hase
1021 84th Ave.	4355 Mockingbird Lane
Oakland, CA 94621-1831	Banning, CA 92220
510-562-6753	951-849-9382

****

The Official Roller Derby Reunion Hotel
Valley Park Hotel
2404 Stevens Creek Blvd., San Jose, CA 95128 (408) 293-5000
1 bed w/ Jacuzzi $74 + tax / 2 beds w/ Jacuzzi $87 + tax

Printed in the United States
By Bookmasters